More Praise for *No More Regrets!*

"This book is the key to unlock a life without regrets that is filled with joy, happiness, and prosperity. Read it, use it, and share it."
—**Harry Paul, coauthor of *Fish!***

"We're all searching for greater happiness, and Marc's heartfelt book provides wonderful tools to help us find it."
—**Barbara Sher, bestselling author of *Wishcraft* and *I C**
Anything If I Only Knew What It Wa

"You don't want your las   ∍ over.'
This book will inspire yo   ) do it
right the first time."
—**John Izzo, author of *Th***   _____ **ver Before**
    You Die

"Marc has done it again. His inspiring words of wisdom will remind you of what is important in your life and help you make decisions so that you too will have no more regrets."
—**Vicki Halsey, author of *Brilliance by Design* and coauthor of *The Hamster Revolution* and *The Hamster Revolution for Meetings***

"*No More Regrets!* is your playbook for living life to its fullest! Everyone benefits from a good coach, and Marc entertainingly leads you through life's most important lessons."
—**Chris Marlowe, 1984 Olympic Gold Medalist and play-by-play announcer for the Denver Nuggets**

"Inspirational, easy to read, and practical. If we don't learn from our past, we are doomed to repeat out mistakes. *No More Regrets!* shows us how to learn and move on so we are free to experience the full and enriched life we desire."
—**Jesse Stoner, coauthor of *Full Steam Ahead!***

No More Regrets!

OTHER BOOKS BY THE AUTHOR

*The Leadership Pill: The Missing Ingredient
in Motivating People Today*
(with Ken Blanchard)

*Naked Management: Bare Essentials for
Managing the X-Generation at Work*

No More Regrets!

30 Ways to Greater Happiness and Meaning in Your Life

Marc Muchnick

BK

Berrett–Koehler Publishers, Inc.
San Francisco
a BK Life book

Copyright © 2011 by People First Group Holdings, LLC

All rights reserved. No part of this publication may be reproduced, distributed, or transmitted in any form or by any means, including photocopying, recording, or other electronic or mechanical methods, without the prior written permission of the publisher, except in the case of brief quotations embodied in critical reviews and certain other noncommercial uses permitted by copyright law. For permission requests, write to the publisher, addressed "Attention: Permissions Coordinator," at the address below.

Berrett-Koehler Publishers, Inc.
235 Montgomery Street, Suite 650
San Francisco, CA 94104-2916
Tel: (415) 288-0260   Fax: (415) 362-2512   www.bkconnection.com

Ordering Information
Quantity sales. Special discounts are available on quantity purchases by corporations, associations, and others. For details, contact the "Special Sales Department" at the Berrett-Koehler address above.
Individual sales. Berrett-Koehler publications are available through most bookstores. They can also be ordered directly from Berrett-Koehler: Tel: (800) 929-2929; Fax: (802) 864-7626; www.bkconnection.com
Orders for college textbook/course adoption use. Please contact Berrett-Koehler: Tel: (800) 929-2929; Fax: (802) 864-7626.
Orders by U.S. trade bookstores and wholesalers. Please contact Ingram Publisher Services, Tel: (800) 509-4887; Fax: (800) 838-1149; E-mail: customer .service@ingrampublisherservices.com; or visit www.ingrampublisherservices.com/ Ordering for details about electronic ordering.

Berrett-Koehler and the BK logo are registered trademarks of Berrett-Koehler Publishers, Inc.

Printed in the United States of America

Berrett-Koehler books are printed on long-lasting acid-free paper. When it is available, we choose paper that has been manufactured by environmentally responsible processes. These may include using trees grown in sustainable forests, incorporating recycled paper, minimizing chlorine in bleaching, or recycling the energy produced at the paper mill.

Library of Congress Cataloging-in-Publication Data
Muchnick, Marc.
  No more regrets! : 30 ways to greater happiness and meaning in your life / Marc Muchnick. — 1st ed.
    p. cm.
  Includes index.
  ISBN 978-1-60509-886-9 (pbk. : alk. paper)
  1. Regret. 2. Satisfaction. 3. Happiness. 4. Self-realization. I. Title.
  BF575.R33M83   2011
  158—dc22   2010037407

FIRST EDITION
16 15 14 13 12 11   10 9 8 7 6 5 4 3 2 1

Cover design: Richard Adelson
Cover art: ©iStockphoto.com/JulyVelchev
Book design and composition: Beverly Butterfield, Girl of the West Productions
Copyediting: PeopleSpeak

This book is dedicated to the following incredible people:

*My wife, Kim, you have been my partner in trying
to live life with no more regrets for over twenty years.
You are truly my rock and best friend.*

*My children, Jessica and Blake, you never cease
to remind me of what's most important in life.
I am so proud of you every day.*

*My parents, who are forever young at heart and
have taught me big lessons in life through their
actions and not just their words. Thank you.*

*My good friend Gary Gotlieb (1966–2009),
you lit up the world and everyone's life that you touched.
I will miss you but never forget you.*

Contents

Foreword

YOU'RE ABOUT TO take a journey: thirty engaging and memorable brief stories will trigger insight into the choices you've made in your life. Not bad choices, not good choices—just choices. Choices that look a little different with the addition of time. Choices that may have caused you to judge yourself and wonder if a different choice would have been better. It's so easy to become self-critical, second-guess our decisions, and agonize over how we'd do things differently if only we could do them over again. What we need is a way to avoid this trap of regret. This is exactly what Marc's book *No More Regrets!* offers, and it has personally helped me recognize the importance of getting rid of regret in my life.

For the last thirty-nine years, I have worked as a teacher, coach, and consultant. While this has brought me much joy and success, I have felt the negative power of regret first-hand. For example, early in my career I was asked to step in as the coach of an aspiring high school tennis team when a colleague of mine suffered a fatal heart attack. We made it to the championship but we lost in the finals, which is an episode I often revisit. I wonder if those young athletes would have won the title if I had made better decisions as the coach. I also think about how, as a young dad, I made some impulsive parenting decisions that fell short of what I expected of myself. In addition, not taking a strong stand on my personal values eventually jeopardized a relationship with my business partner, whom I truly cared about. Each of these experiences left me feeling like a victim of regret and for a period of time interfered with my self-confidence as well as my ability to continue to learn and grow and be the difference maker I wanted to be.

After reading just a few chapters of *No More Regrets!*, I was struck by a revelation: there is actually a way to avoid regrets. Remember those times when the light bulb went on in your head and all of a sudden you "got it"? That is the experience I had when I read this book. It became clearer to me that while we all have regrets, we are capable of moving past them and putting an end to regret in the future. Personal integrity in my actions and in my decision making will never be easy, but it's possible and ultimately a choice that I have the power to make. If I can learn to live the values I say I profess, I will still make mistakes but I will have no more regrets. I encourage you to reread this book many times as I have and share it with your friends, family, and coworkers. Enjoy the journey.

Tom Champoux
Founder and President, The Effectiveness Institute

Acknowledgments

I WOULD LIKE to thank the following amazing people for helping me make this book a reality—I am forever grateful to you and will always cherish your friendship, uniqueness, inspiration, and support: Mo, Slick, Rye, Johnny Scribner, Vish, Dr. Q Taylor, Nicole and Uncle Matty, Mark and Maxine Rossman, Adam and Cindy, Dana and Eddy, Julie and Gordo, the Becks, Dana, "Boom-Boom" D and John, Larry and Shari, Steven and Sheri, Cousin Jason and the Dorks, Tom and Emily, Chipsters and Nina, J. Garcia, The Men's Club Dudes, Steve Jensen, Big Bob Moehler, Tom Champoux, Ken Blanchard, Madeleine Blanchard, "Big Will" Moreland, Mrs. Madden, Mrs. Keebey, Tim Haggstrom, Dave and Flo Wagner, Lloyd Bachrach, Principal Stevens, Wally Armstrong, Harry "The Fish Guy" Paul, Chinacat Rubinski, Neil "Laz" Lazaroff, Margolis, Norm and Liz Feinberg, Judy Dubin, John Whitlock, Johnny Lampitt, Marty Goodman, Andrew Donner, Mimi Gotlieb, Debbie Greenberg, Andrea Stein, Neil Camberg, Steve Piersanti, and the entire BK Gang!

Introduction

You only live once, but if you do it right,
once is enough.

MAE WEST

NONE OF US want to look back on life with regrets or to
be that person who reflects on the past and says, "If only
I would have spent more quality time with the people I
love most in my life . . ." "If only I would have taken that
vacation instead of working so much . . . " "If only I would
have gone with my gut . . . " "If only I could take back
what I said . . . " But how often does that person sound a
lot like you and me?

Gary's Gift

Not too long ago a good friend of mine passed away—
he was in his early forties and left a lot of loving friends
and family behind. Gary's battle with cancer lasted several
years, and during that time I learned what a true fighter
he was. When he was first diagnosed, the doctors told him
he had only a few months to live. But Gary refused to give
up and remained dedicated to working hard, traveling,
and most of all spending quality time with his children in
the midst of grueling chemotherapy regimens. Gary had

always lived life to the fullest and was a shining example of how to seize the day and live in the moment.

Six months before he died, Gary came to visit me. We sat on the back patio enjoying the beautiful summer day and reminiscing about old times. But when I asked Gary how he was feeling, he didn't want to talk about it. Instead he asked me lots of questions—what my family had planned for vacation, how work was going, and what my dreams were for the future. Then he asked what my biggest regret was.

"My *biggest* regret?" I repeated.

"Yes. If there was one thing in your life that you could go back and do differently, what would it be?" he clarified.

"I need more time to think about it," I replied, "but since you brought it up, what's *your* biggest regret?"

I watched Gary's tired face grow tormented in the uncomfortable silence that followed. Finally he spoke. "There was a girl I dated many years ago . . . I should have never let her go." Gary paused, then said, "She was my soul mate, yet I didn't realize it until twenty-three years later. When I got sick, she started calling me in the hospital. It was then that I realized what a deep connection she and I had, one that I somehow failed to recognize when I knew her back in college. I can't help but wonder how my life would have been different with her in it, and I kick myself because now it's too late. When people say that life is short, I literally know what they mean. As my longtime friend, you must promise me that you'll always do your best to live *your* life without any more regrets. For that you will always thank me." Gary hugged me, and I knew it was the last time I would ever have the opportunity to spend a quality afternoon with him.

Three things became clearer to me on that day than ever before:

- We all have regrets.

- Our regrets go with us to the grave.

- There is no time like the present to start living life without any more of them.

This wake-up call was Gary's gift to me and one I now want to give to you. The choices we make in life, as well as the missed opportunities, have a profound impact on our happiness in the end. To start working toward the goal of a life with no more regrets, we first have to understand what regrets are and why we have them in the first place.

What Are Regrets?

My definition of regrets is as follows:

Regrets are the things we do that we wish we hadn't done *and* the things we fail to do that we wish we had done, both of which result in unhappiness, disappointment, or remorse.

In other words, regrets are all about our actions and inactions. Therefore, regrets are about our behaviors and the feelings of unhappiness, disappointment, or remorse we attach to those behaviors. For example, if you've ever broken a promise, acted inconsistently with your values, made poor choices, or hurt someone as a result of what you've said or done (or failed to say or do), it was your *behaviors* that led to your feelings of regret.

Understanding regret as a product of our behaviors has direct implications for how we make decisions. Typically we bring a number of elements into our decision-making framework, such as timing, context, opportunity, cost, how we'll feel about the decision after it is made, what the impact will be, and so on.

What this book brings to the table is that for every decision we make, we must *also* ask the following two behavioral questions as a standard part of our decision-making process:

- Will I have regrets if I do it (or don't do it)?

- Will I avoid having regrets if I do it (or don't do it)?

For example, will it cause a fight with my wife? Will I cut it too close to make it to my destination? Will he forgive me if I do it? If I don't speak up now, will I regret it forever? The takeaway here is that many of the decisions we make need to take into account the regret factor. Be sure to ask yourself these two behavior-focused questions as you make decisions going forward if you want to have a life with no more regrets.

Keep in mind that regrets are not necessarily the same as mistakes. We can learn a lot from our mistakes, but we don't necessarily have to regret them. In fact, some of the best lessons in life come from making mistakes. Essentially, our regrets and our mistakes can differ by the positive or negative feelings we attribute to them. While we will all make mistakes, the key is to avoid making mistakes that we ultimately regret.

One additional aspect of understanding regrets is that our regrets have some common themes, though the sources of our individual regrets are unique to each of us:

- We get stuck in ruts and become prisoners to our regrets.
- We take some things or people for granted.
- We sacrifice our authenticity.
- We stop growing, learning, and evolving.
- We become overly self-absorbed, insensitive, and judgmental.

What This Book Offers

The thirty ways to greater happiness and meaning that I present to you in this book are divided into five overarching strategies for having no more regrets, each of which is based on an identified theme of regret:

1. Get out of your rut.
2. Take nothing for granted.
3. Aim for authenticity.
4. Stretch yourself.
5. Be a force of goodness.

I am confident that out of the thirty ways I offer for living life with no more regrets, at least a few chapters will really resonate with you. Just one or two new insights can be the key to greater happiness and meaning in your life, career, and relationships. In other words, choosing just one action or new way of doing things can lead to a potentially life-changing moment. For example, when you're stuck in a rut, learning a new way to look at that situation might help you get out of the rut and change your trajectory. Likewise, if you view yourself as being a victim of your circumstances, focusing on what is within your control is empowering and can make you realize that you can break out of this state of mind.

Making the Most of This Book

So here's how to use this book: first, you can use it for yourself, at work, in your career, with your family, or in your relationships. As you are reading each chapter, evaluate how well the message fits for you. If it's a good fit, ask the following:

- What insights does it provide?

- What does it inspire you to stop doing or start doing?

- How will this impact your life?

Next, for a chapter that you feel would be a better fit for someone else in your life, be sure to share it with that person and encourage him or her to take action. Then move on to the next chapter because the key to living *your* life with no more regrets is there, just waiting to be revealed. At the back of the book, I've also provided easy-to-follow next steps for taking action along with a No More Regrets! Game Plan tool that I think you will find useful.

Finally, make "No More Regrets!" both your credo and your commitment for the future—avoid repeating past regrets and prevent new ones from occurring. Following are my stories, many of them personal, about what it means to do just that. My goal is to get you to reflect on your *own* stories of when you've been stuck in a rut, taken something or someone for granted, struggled with being authentic, stopped growing or learning, or needed a reminder of how to be a force of goodness in the world. I encourage you to share these experiences with me and a growing community of enthusiastic readers on the official book Web site: http://www.no-more-regrets.com.

I look forward to hearing from you!

None of us want to
look back on life
with regrets.

*~What is your biggest regret in life and
how did it impact you?*

PART ONE
Get Out of Your Rut

Stop Doing What Isn't Working

NOT TOO LONG after we got married, my wife and I got into a rut. We were working dead-end jobs for bosses we didn't like and were barely making enough money to pay the monthly bills. We were happy as a couple, yet we were unhappy with our professional lives. Between the two of us, we had racked up more than six figures in student loan debt. In addition, we had moved to an area of town that was more affordable and closer to our jobs, but this had taken us farther away from our friends and the coastal part of San Diego we loved most. Despite our best efforts, we couldn't see how our situation was going to change any time soon.

I started teaching at two community colleges in the evenings to supplement the income from both of our full-time jobs. We also started selling personalized gifts at the local flea market—not exactly our strong suit, but my wife had a knack for calligraphy and I was decent at sales. Every weekend we'd haul display cases, folding tables and chairs, and all of our products in the back of my tiny convertible to our even tinier booth at the swap meet. It was quite a spectacle and an exhausting process. More than anything, though, we regretted the fact that we were working so hard and had so little to show for it.

One unseasonably hot Saturday after spending eight hours on the asphalt-paved flea market lot, we'd finally had enough. We were poor, stressed, and miserable. We were tired of trying to manage our odd jobs on top of our real jobs and still getting nowhere. It just wasn't working! After a long talk that night, we agreed we needed to make a drastic change. We got out a map and decided that we were going to move to a place where it was much cheaper to live. While we hated to leave San Diego, we knew that one day we'd come back on our own terms when it was the right time.

Starting our new life adventure was an incredibly liberating experience. We resigned from our jobs and shut down our personalized gift business. We set new professional and personal goals. We worked out the logistics of moving and got excited about the future. What quickly became clear to us is that when you stop doing what isn't working, you free up enormous amounts of creative, productive energy and liberate yourself from the shadow of regret.

Within a year after moving, we were able to get ourselves financially back on our feet and in active pursuit of our professional goals. I started writing my first book and worked on getting a consulting business off the ground while my wife was busy running a children's nonprofit charity organization. The following year we were finally able to buy our first house, and soon after that we welcomed our first child into the world. We encountered plenty of obstacles along the way, but we just felt happier and more in control of our own lives.

Don't expect life to be any different if you keep doing what you've always done. Whether you're in a bad relationship, the wrong job, or a place in your life where you feel stuck, have the courage to shake things up and cut your losses. Free yourself from the regret of the situation you're in and take a new direction. Stop doing what isn't working so you can start doing what works.

Stop doing what isn't working so you can start doing what works.

— *What in your life are you doing that isn't working right now?*

— *If you stopped doing it, what would happen?*

2

Pick a Place to Start

EVERY JANUARY 1 we engage in the long-standing ritual of making our New Year's resolutions. Some of us actually write them down; others just commit them to memory. In addition, some of us postpone the exercise indefinitely despite our best intentions. But all of us go through the process of at least *thinking* about what we should put on the list of goals we hope to accomplish in the coming year. Historical favorites include losing weight, earning more money, getting a different job, making new friends, creating greater work-life balance, putting old photos into a scrapbook, eating healthier foods, taking a longer vacation, exercising more, and procrastinating less.

The problem of course with most of our "to do" lists—whether they include our yearly resolutions, tasks at work, or things we need to get done around the house—is that we put too much on them. It's not too long before the stark realization sets in: we may never get everything done. This can be overwhelming and ultimately lead to feelings of regret if we don't complete the entire list or if we don't give it our best effort because we are trying to do too many things at once. Regret may also be the result if we spend so much time overanalyzing how to get it all done that we wind up getting little or nothing done.

So where do we start? Several years ago a man named Lee Staggert called me about getting some personal coaching on how to better organize his life. Specifically, he wanted to increase his effectiveness in accomplishing his daily tasks so he could focus more on working toward his goals for the future. Lee was the type of person who was used to feeling like he could accomplish anything he set out to do, but lately he had been falling behind. As an example, he was receiving over one hundred e-mails a day and getting to only the ten or so that were the highest priority. The rest of them just sat in his in-box and accumulated throughout the month, leaving him with literally thousands of unopened e-mails that he'd purge on the first of the next month in order to give himself the illusion of a fresh start. Clearly this did not solve the problem and was only making it worse.

Beyond that, Lee was up against the clock to fill two vacant positions in his office in the midst of trying to grow a new business venture. He was also required to attend a barrage of daily meetings, which just sucked up more of his time. Finally, he was finding less and less quality time to spend with his family since each night he brought home work that he couldn't get done at the office. It may come as no surprise that Lee was stressed, overwhelmed, and frustrated.

My counsel to Lee was simple: "Pick a place to start," I said. "Choose one thing on your 'to do' list that will be a big source of regret for you until it gets resolved."

"What about all the rest?" Lee asked.

"It's not like you're going to forget about the other items on the list," I reassured him. "You're just going to find a starting point where you'll put the greatest focus for the time being. The problem right now is that you've got so much on your list, you don't know where to begin."

While Lee wasn't completely sold on my advice, he said he'd give it a try and chose to start with e-mails. His initial goal was to cut his end-of-month unopened e-mail load in half by setting aside "e-mail elimination time" twice a week for one hour a shot. In just four weeks, however, Lee wound up reducing his unopened e-mails by 70 percent. By the end of the following month, he was down 85 percent! Becoming more efficient at managing his e-mail load also allowed him to spend more time targeting the next items on the list. It wasn't long before he had freed himself from the regret of feeling ineffective and overwhelmed.

It's better to do one thing well as opposed to a lot of things poorly. When tackling your own "to do" list, don't try to take it all on at once. Instead, consider which item on the list will give you the greatest sense of satisfaction and return on your time investment once addressed. Then choose a starting point so you can begin working toward success. This will help you feel energized because you'll have a strategy in place for moving forward. Pick a place to start and you will no longer feel stuck.

Pick a place to
start and you will
no longer feel stuck.

— What does your current "to do" list look like?

*— If you had to pick a place to start, which
item on the list would you choose and why?*

3

Make Peace with Yourself

MY SON, BLAKE, was born in the middle of a hurricane, literally as the eye of the storm passed over the hospital where my wife was giving birth. It was a scene that can only be described as chaotic: the hospital was already on backup generators due to flooding and a power outage, and we were on the only floor that hadn't been evacuated yet. Nurses were running around frantically as my wife begged for an epidural. Then, just as she was about to deliver, the doctor informed us that the umbilical cord was wrapped around our baby's neck. As he tried to remedy the situation, I could see signs of panic on his face. He reassured us that everything was fine, but our son was a deep blue color upon coming out of the womb.

All I remember is pleading to God to let this baby breathe. I can say without hesitation that I have never been so happy to hear a baby cry his lungs out. At that moment, I knew my son was resilient and determined to put up a fight, though I still wondered what impact the early trauma might have had on him. Did he stop breathing for too long? Would he be "normal"? I hated to think that way, but I kept torturing myself with the unknown.

As my son grew from an infant to a toddler, I continued to worry about him, even though his cognitive, social, and physical development was fine. Instead of celebrating his good health, I focused more on possible reasons for concern: he had chronic eczema that made him scratch his skin until it bled, he developed a severe nut allergy that resulted in a 911 call and a trip to the emergency room, he got bronchitis more frequently than most kids, and he needed breathing treatments for wheezing. Right or wrong, I attributed these symptoms to his precarious situation at birth, not to mention I couldn't shake the idea—however illogical—that I was partly responsible. Perhaps I could have done something to prevent the umbilical cord from getting wrapped around his neck. Maybe I should have moved my wife to a different hospital that wasn't in the direct path of a hurricane. I was haunted with regret every time I relived the experience in my head.

When Blake was almost five we took a family trip to Portland, and the itinerary included a visit to the famous outdoor market. Blake was insistent upon having his palm read by a woman at a table full of tarot cards, despite my attempts to lure him toward the cotton candy booth. Reluctantly I conceded, terrified that the palm reader might reveal something awful to my son about his health. At the conclusion of the reading my son called me over. To my surprise, he was all smiles. Then he ran off to find Mom while I paid the bill.

As I started to reach for my wallet, the palm reader grabbed me by the arm and stared into my eyes with captivating intensity. "You don't have to worry about him anymore," she said. "What happened to your son was a long time ago; he's going to be fine now. You can stop worrying, you'll see."

My jaw dropped. How did she know my secret? How did she know he was going to be okay? For some strange reason that I still can't explain, I believed her. Perhaps the sole reason our paths had crossed that day was for her to tell me that a guardian angel was watching over my son. The sense of relief I felt was overwhelming. I broke down crying right there in the middle of the crowded street, overcome with emotion and the revelation that I was no longer a prisoner to my feelings of worry and regret.

Regret can have a powerful hold on us—the key is learning how to release yourself from its grip. I believe my son was born in a hurricane because he can weather any storm. He is healthy, happy, smart, friendly, funny, courageous, athletic, and strong. I am no longer burdened with the weight of regret because I have let go of my emotional baggage from the circumstances of his birth. When we face what torments us, we put a stop to our inner turmoil. Give yourself permission to be imperfect. Come to terms with your feelings of regret and don't beat yourself up over situations you can't control. Make peace with yourself and set yourself free from the past.

Make peace with yourself and set yourself free from the past.

~ *What from your past is still a source of inner turmoil?*

~ *How will you make peace with yourself about this?*

Turn Adversity into Opportunity

SOMETIMES LIFE THROWS us challenges that test our resilience and threaten to keep us stuck in a rut of regret. Lloyd Bachrach knows this all too well: he was born with a congenital bone deficiency that made his lower limbs so unusually small that doctors told his parents he should be institutionalized. When his parents insisted that they were going to take him home, they were warned that he would never be able to have a normal life. "He'll find his way," his parents responded.

Lloyd's parents encouraged him early on to figure out how to do things on his own and refused to coddle him. To the amazement of his doctors, he learned how to crawl without the use of his legs. He became progressively mobile and, despite his severe disability, attended public school when he became school age. Lloyd's attitude from the beginning was one of no regrets for the cards he'd been dealt in life. "You can't miss something you never had," he'd say. Lloyd also adopted a motto that embodied his

can-do approach: "It doesn't matter what you don't have—
just use what you *do* have to pursue your goals."

Lloyd's goals included becoming a top athlete. He developed his upper-body strength by swimming, and then he learned to play baseball. Although he couldn't run very fast on his small legs, he taught himself to scoot around the bases at lightning speed by using only his arms and dragging his legs behind him. Then he took on gymnastics and was a serious competitor throughout high school, so much so that in his senior year he placed fifth in the state tournament. When asked how someone who was a disabled person could be such a formidable opponent to other able-bodied athletes, Lloyd said, "I'm not *dis*abled, I'm *differently* abled." The apex of his athletic career, though, was when he played on the USA sit-volleyball team in the 1996 Paralympics in Atlanta. Now Lloyd, who is married and has two daughters, is a frequent motivational speaker at schools and organizations.

Lloyd's incredible story is a testament to his no-regrets attitude and tenacity around turning his adverse situation into an opportunity. Instead of using his disability as a source of regret, he has used it as a reason to do things that others never suspected he could accomplish. This has implications for people without disabilities as well. For instance, we all have found ourselves in situations where we were at a disadvantage, whether we were vying for a job when other applicants were more qualified, taking a class in school that wasn't in our strong suit, or playing in a competition where the opponent was more skilled. Do we get mired in regret about the fact that we are at a disadvantage, or do we look for creative ways to play to our strengths?

The next time you are confronted with adversity, think about how you can turn it into an opportunity. Consider your unique gifts and be innovative in finding solutions. Look at the possibility for success as opposed to the chance for failure. Believe in yourself and have the confidence to embrace the situation. Turn adversity into an opportunity and face your challenges head-on.

Turn adversity
into an opportunity
and face your
challenges head-on.

*~ What is one aspect of your life where you are
at a disadvantage compared to others?*

~ How can you turn this into an opportunity?

5

Avoid Victimitis

WHEN I WAS in eighth grade I joined a youth group, and at
our first event we had a speaker who introduced us to the
PLUM game. PLUM stood for "Poor Little Unfortunate
Me," and the speaker's contention was that most of us
knew how to play this game all too well, especially when
we were faced with tough challenges or if things didn't go
our way. He explained that when people play the PLUM
game, they take little or no responsibility for their own
situation. Instead they pretend to be victims when actually
they're just whining about their regrets—for example, how
they don't get what they rightfully deserve, how things
never go their way, how they always get the short end of
the stick, and all the other ways that life has somehow
cheated them.

He called this pattern of behavior "victimitis" and was
quick to make the distinction between it and being a true
victim: "People with this condition actually have the ability to change their circumstances," he said, "but somehow
they convince themselves that they can't." Next he had

us practice whining "Poor little unfortunate me!" in our most nasal voice possible. This way he could be certain we understood just how annoying people with this disease sounded. Then he gave some examples of the regrets that adolescents with victimitis whine about, most of which rang true for our group: "I got a bad grade on the test . . ." "I didn't make the team . . ." "I didn't get the part I wanted in the play . . ." "I'm not popular . . ." "My parents are on my case . . ." "I'm grounded for a week . . ." After each example we had to shout "Poor little unfortunate me!" The exercise was both invigorating and revealing, and it still sticks with me today.

I've noticed that adults are also good at playing the PLUM game. Adults with victimitis feel cheated in life and love to whine about their regrets. Familiar whines include "I don't get enough credit for all the work I do around here . . ." "I'll never be able to make enough money to live the life I want . . ." "Everyone else has it easier than me . . ." "I'm overweight . . ." "People take me for granted . . ." "No one understands me . . ." "I'm such a screwup . . ." People with this condition are filled with self-pity and wear their regrets on their sleeves. They are paralyzed by their victimitis and never seem to take ownership of their situation. Plus they're not very fun to be around.

So how do we avoid victimitis? A good way to start is by acknowledging that each of us has the power to change the way we react to the situations we face in life. For instance, if you're having a bad day, feeling dissatisfied with your job, experiencing relationship issues, or failing to live up to your commitments, how you handle these situations is still completely up to you. Look inward instead of outward to identify the true source of your regrets. Refrain from blaming others, making excuses, and acting helpless. If you catch yourself whining, stop. Take personal responsibility for your situation—and also for the solution. When we stop feeling sorry for ourselves, our feelings of regret about our circumstances in life subside. Avoid victimitis and see the world in a better way.

Recognize that each
of us has the power to
change the way we react
to the situations
we face in life.

~ *What is an example of a time when you've shown symptoms of victimitis?*

~ *What can you do going forward to avoid falling into that trap again?*

6

Steer Clear of Toxic People

SOME PEOPLE WILL squeeze the life out of you if you let them. They're the ones who are quick to criticize us and make callous remarks behind our backs. They thrive on pointing out our inadequacies and love to remind us of our flaws. They like to prey on us when we're most vulnerable and kick us when we're down. In addition, they relish the moments when we are vulnerable and take every opportunity to chip away at our self-esteem. Deep down, they are insecure, unhappy folks who have discovered they feel better about themselves when others feel worse. Warning: steer clear of these toxic people—they are poster children for regret and reek of negativity.

Instead, surround yourself with positive, supportive people who will encourage you and believe in you. These are individuals who tend to smile a lot, love to laugh at life, and are always there to cheer you on. They see your potential even when you're not showing it, and they look at every day as an opportunity for you to do something great. They are also the ones who boost your confidence when you're up against a challenge and who lift your spirits when you're down in the dumps or stuck in a rut. They are eternal optimists and die-hard advocates. They've got your back and will always be in your corner.

Wendy, the senior vice president of human resources at a large company I worked at early in my career, was not one of these positive and supportive people. She was a virtual tyrant who was referred to as Toxic Wendy throughout employee circles and was notorious for her sharp tongue, cruel wit, and abusive style. She took pride in publicly humiliating people and then discrediting them behind their backs the minute they left the room. Her job title gave her power and she abused it at every opportunity. It was not uncommon for her staff to walk out of her office crying after she had flown into a sudden tirade while scrutinizing their work. She literally went through a new secretary every other month—two of them had to take stress leave due to the harsh reprimands and cutting remarks Wendy doled out to them on a daily basis.

In my exit interview from the company, I met with the CEO, who asked me why I was leaving. My response was straight to the point: "I'd regret it if I stayed one more day. I think you'll see a lot more people leaving as well if you keep the head of Human Resources around. No one deserves that kind of abuse. The crazy thing is that she's the one in charge of people!" A few months later I got a call from one of my former coworkers, who told me that

Toxic Wendy had gotten the boot in the midst of a nasty ethics scandal. While perhaps justice had been served, the damage she had done could not be erased.

Hanging around toxic people is a recipe for regret. Get them out of your life and stay as far away from them as possible. Instead, surround yourself with positive people. Just being around them will make you feel more energized, motivated, confident, inspired, happy, and alive. Steer clear of toxic people and put yourself in the presence of the people who bring out the best in you.

Steer clear of toxic people and put yourself in the presence of the people who bring out the best in you.

— *Who are the toxic people in your life?*

— *How do you feel when you're around them versus people who bring out the best in you?*

PART TWO
Take Nothing for Granted

7

Live Your Life the Way You Want to Be Remembered

WHEN I WAS first told that I had melanoma, my immediate reaction was denial—there must have been some mistake. After all, I wore sunscreen religiously, I was in reasonably good physical condition, and I definitely did not feel sick. But once the doctor repeated my diagnosis and underscored how I absolutely needed to come in for surgery the next morning at 8:00 a.m., I just stood there in shock.

Suddenly a flood of memories raced through my head as I contemplated the prospect of dying and whether or not I had lived my life thus far the way I wanted to be remembered. For instance, how many times had I promised my kids that I'd spend quality time with them only to get caught up doing something else? How many times had I forgotten to tell my wife that I love her and appreciate everything that she does? How many times had I vowed to keep in more frequent contact with my closest friends only to let life get in the way again? And how many times had I gotten so caught up in work that it began to rule my life? These regrets and others haunted me as I continued to ponder my fate.

The next morning I went in for surgery and prayed. As I was being taken into the operating room I promised myself that should the procedure be successful, I would commit to doing a better job of living my life the way I wanted to be remembered. Furthermore, I was resolute that I wouldn't allow myself to have any more of the regrets I'd experienced in the past. Fortunately when the lab reports came back a week later, it was good news: the cancer had not spread. I was so grateful to have this new lease on life and the opportunity to start working on my personal improvement plan.

Within just a couple of weeks I began to see progress. I was doing a better job of keeping my promises to my kids and spending more quality time with them. I was also showing greater appreciation to my wife and even started having a weekly "date night" with her. In addition, I made it a priority to pick up the phone more to call my friends and tried to create a better balance between my work life and home life. While all of this is still a work in progress today, it feels good not to have those same feelings of regret that I had before.

Life can change in an instant—we all need to realize that. Cherish each day and work at being the best version of you. Take note of the gaps between the person you are today and the person that you hope to be. What changes will you make? What will you do more of or less of? What will you start doing and stop doing? Don't wait for tomorrow to live your life the way you want to be remembered today.

Don't wait for tomorrow to live your life the way you want to be remembered today.

~ *How do you want your life to be remembered?*

~ *What will you start doing today to live more in line with that image?*

8

Greet the Day

THERE ARE TWO types of people in the world: those who greet the day and those who wake up on the wrong side of the bed. My wife is the consummate example of someone who truly wakes up every morning and says, "Hello world, it's going to be a great day!" She's cheery, smiley, and full of energy from the moment she rises, ready to take on whatever life throws her way. What intrigues me most, though, is that she actually *expects* her day to go well from the beginning. She believes with all her heart that when you greet the day, you have fewer regrets in life because you've already started your day off feeling happy and inspired.

Then there are those of us—like me—who are just the opposite. We'd prefer to sleep late and absolutely cringe when the alarm clock goes off (the first time). We dread getting up and when we finally do, we're grumpy. People who know us steer clear until we've had our first cup of coffee. Invariably, the quest to avoid regrets is a daily battle for us since each day we tend to start things off on the wrong foot.

You might conclude at this point that being good at greeting the day is a function of personality and that it all depends on how our personalities are wired. While this may be true to some extent, what I've come to realize is that greeting the day is also grounded in tangible behaviors that every one of us can learn to adopt. In other words, hope exists for us all! The key is to figure out what works best for you as an individual and then create a morning routine that eventually becomes a matter of habit.

Following are a few simple tips that you may want to experiment with as you think about how you'd like to greet the day. First, try waking up to your favorite music instead of the annoying beep or buzz of an alarm clock—today's technology makes this quite easy and you don't have to spend a fortune. Then make your bed so you feel productive right out of the gate—as trivial as this might seem, it works. Next, do some light exercise to get the blood flowing, even if you just run in place or do jumping jacks for five minutes—you'll be surprised at what an instant burst of energy this gives you. Finally, eat something healthy—this will help stave off midmorning burnout. Any combination of these strategies for greeting the day, as well as others that you might want to add, will help put your body and brain into gear and get you into a no-regrets frame of mind more quickly.

Life is too short to wake up with a frown. If greeting the day is a formula for happiness—and if happiness is essentially the state of having no regrets—then it makes good sense to make greeting the day a priority. While we can't do much to change how we're wired, we *can* change how we begin each morning. Greet the day and see how it improves your outlook on life.

Greet the day and
see how it improves
your outlook on life.

— Do you tend to start the day with a smile
or a frown?

— What are some specific ways to improve on
how you greet the day?

9

Stay in Touch

AT SOME POINT in life we begin to realize that maintaining friendships gets harder and harder. Like it or not, we all get busy and sometimes just don't have enough time to keep up with everything—and everyone—in our world. Before we know it, we may start to grow distant from people we used to be close to and eventually lose track of their lives. Without frequency of interaction, our friendships can wither and fade, and for that we may wind up having regrets.

To keep your relationships alive, you must take the time to stay in touch. This requires conscious effort and is not always convenient or easy. Essentially, it means either being a good communicator or learning to become one. In other words, we have to take the initiative to find out what's going on in other people's lives and be willing to let them in on what's happening in our world as well. The mere fact that our lives are so overscheduled and fast paced calls for creativity in our quest to stay in touch.

Dan Vishny is someone who knows how to step outside the box when it comes to staying in touch. Vish, as he prefers to be called, is an accountant by training who also has a penchant for vegan cooking and travel. One day Vish, while living in Chicago, was experimenting with a new vegan recipe when he got a call from a friend he used to cook with back in Eugene, Oregon. Although it was great to catch up, Vish was saddened by the fact that many of his closest friends were spread out across the country and that he hardly ever talked to them anymore. In addition, due to his busy work schedule and the pressures of raising a family, it was always either the wrong time to go visit or just too expensive.

Finally Vish decided that enough was enough. He made it his mission within the coming year to pay a personal house call to as many of the people he loved in life as he could, and he was determined to do it on a shoestring budget over a thirty-day period. Step one: he started saving money and his vacation days at work—even though he only got a few weeks off a year, the combination of sick leave and personal days would get him pretty close to what he needed. Step two: a few months later he bought a used recreational vehicle on eBay at a fire sale price with the money he had saved. Step three: he started making a month's worth of veggie burritos to eliminate the lion's share of food expenses for his family on the trip. Step four: he e-mailed his friends and told them to be on the lookout for a beat-up RV with Illinois plates.

The trip was an incredible experience for both his family and the friends that they visited from coast to coast. Friendships were rekindled and the way was paved for future reunions. Through Vish's determination to stay in touch, what was initially a source of pain and regret had turned into a wellspring of happiness and reconnection.

The good news is that there are plenty of simple and easy things you can do to stay in touch. Start by remembering birthdays. Mail care packages and send updates on your life. Text a quick hello or "thinking of you" note. Chat on Facebook and leverage other social networking tools to connect with people you haven't talked to for a while. Share traditions. Go for a weekend getaway together. Get on Skype. Return each other's phone calls. Send recent pictures. Meet after work or take morning walks together if you live in the same town. Set a designated time to talk each week. Celebrate life events together. Show up unexpectedly. Plan a reunion. More than anything, be the friend that you want others to be. Remember that it's never too late to start, regardless of how long it's been since you've last talked.

Life can get in the way of relationships, and that can lead to regret. Commit to ensuring your friends don't feel "de-prioritized" or taken for granted. Reach out regularly to the important people in your life and strengthen the lines of communication. Be tenacious about finding ways to get quality time with each other, even if it's not in person or as frequent as you would like. Make a conscious effort to stay in touch. Nurture your relationships and see how they blossom.

Nurture your
relationships and
see how they blossom.

~ *Which of your relationships are in need of greater nurturing?*

~ *What will you do to stay in touch?*

Make Every Day Count

OUR DAYS ARE numbered. No matter how hard we try to prolong our time on earth, the reality is that we are mere mortals and will not live forever. Although we may fantasize about what it would be like to relive the past, ultimately we must figure out how to make the most of our time while we are here in the living present. Each moment we waste is a potential source of regret and literally time lost.

The question we have to ask ourselves is, "Are we passengers on a journey through time or are we explorers on a mission of discovery?" In the latter case, each day is an opportunity to embrace life as active participants rather than as casual observers. Instead of being aloof and detached, we must get engaged and make every day count. Likewise, as opposed to remaining ambivalent, we need to be deliberate about how we spend our time. Sitting on the sidelines and watching life from afar will only result in apathy and regret.

Several summers ago my grandmother, whom we called Gigi, passed away after a long and happy life of ninety-one

years. No o_
Gigi. Until tl
cal activist, an
and loved to la
family member
ful, thoughtful,
event near or far
At 6:00 a.m. each
go, prepared to le_
finished until Gigi

What fascinated _____ talked about death withou_ ____ _eluctance. She made it clear that because she made every day count, she would have no regrets when she died. I can't even begin to count the times I heard her in perfect health utter the words "When I'm dead and gone I won't regret a thing" as she spoke openly about what she was going to bequeath everyone.

Less than a year before Gigi died, she flew across the country to come visit us. Her health was noticeably deteriorating, but she still had her wits about her. When I asked how she was feeling, she gave me a response that I'll never forget. "Don't worry about me, darling—I've lived a great life," she said defiantly. "I've traveled. I was married to an amazing man. I have twenty-two wonderful grandchildren and great-grandchildren, plus I have twice as many nieces and nephews. I've had good health and lots of happiness. Really, now, what more could you possibly ask for? I've seen it all and done it all! So when I die, don't you dare cry

my life and waste your tears. I'll
use I've lived every day to the fullest."
day count is something that each of us
ever, it requires more than just well-intended
for it to become a reality. It takes effort, dedica-
, a thirst for adventure, and the resolve to get actively
involved in life as opposed to watching it pass us by.

You have only one life to live, so start living it. Strive to make the most of each day. Live with unbridled passion and enthusiasm. Find ways to make your day more memorable and worthwhile. Get involved in a cause that's important to you. Go to places you haven't been before. Hang out with people you actually enjoy spending time with. Splurge every once in a while. Be curious and keep learning. Laugh out loud. Make every day count so you get the most out of what life has to offer.

Make every day count
so you get the most out of
what life has to offer.

~ *What will you do to make every day count?*

~ *What challenges will you face in making this happen?*

Freeze the Moment

LIFE IS FULL of magical moments, not all of which can be photographed, videotaped, or digitized. One way to preserve special experiences that you'd regret forgetting is to "freeze the moment"—to take an intentional mental picture of everything you see, hear, sense, and feel at a particular juncture in time and then permanently commit it to memory. A "freezable moment" is the split second of joy, beauty, laughter, irony, celebration, mystery, intrigue, exhilaration, wonder, or grace that makes us feel at one with the universe. It's the flash of inspiration that reassures us life is worth living if only to have been alive at that exact instant.

Some of my top freezable moments include the first time I saw the incredible Pacific sunset, the moment I met my future wife, the day I got accepted into graduate school and my grandpa told me how proud he was of me, the many times I've laughed so hard with my best friends that my stomach ached, and the afternoon I watched the

Grateful Dead play one of the most amazing sets ever at Frost Amphitheater.

Favorite freezable moments also include seeing the vibrant turquoise color of the water in Tahiti, experiencing the bliss of getting lost in Venice, noticing the way the mountains turn purple in Lake Arrowhead as daylight fades, hearing my wife say "I love you" to me for the very first time and then "I do" when we got married, holding my children just minutes after each of them was born, seeing our old dog Scruffy hoarding all of our covers in the middle of the night as if she owned the bed, feeling the exhilaration and exhaustion as I crossed the finish line in the only marathon I'll probably ever run, watching the look on my son's face when he came into the ballgame with bases loaded and no outs and then pitched a scoreless inning, and savoring the way my daughter still becomes a little girl again every time I tuck her in and say goodnight.

Beyond relying on memory or the use of a camera or video recorder, you can freeze the moment in a number of other ways. For instance, you can write down a detailed description of the freezable moment in a journal or you can simply call someone and tell him or her about it. Alternatively, you can share it with others via e-mail or on a social networking site. In addition, you can set aside time to memorialize this special moment through a celebration or by developing your own traditions.

Make a conscious effort to imprint your life's most amazing moments forever in your mind so you'll never have the regret of forgetting them. By preserving the memories of these snapshots in time, you can go back and experience them again and again. While you can't turn back the clock, you can always revisit the best times of your life when you learn to freeze the moment.

Freeze the moment
so you can always revisit
the best times of
your life.

～ *What are some of your favorite "freezable moments"?*

～ *What made them so memorable?*

12

Put Your Stuff
in Perspective

IT'S AMAZING HOW attached we've become to our "stuff" in life. Imagine if you had to give up your cell phone or your computer or your iPod or your high-definition television. As much as we hate to admit it, our happiness is often tied to our gadgets, conveniences, and material possessions. Sometimes we get so consumed with our things that we need a wake-up call to gain perspective.

Several years ago my family was unexpectedly forced to evacuate our home at 5:30 a.m. Wildfires in the surrounding area had started burning out of control and the wind was picking up. As we raced to pack our most precious possessions, ash was pouring down from the sky and blowing all over our yard.

It quickly dawned on us that we didn't have enough room in the car to bring everything we owned with us. In fifteen minutes or less and with limited capacity for luggage, what do you take? We scrambled to find our passports, laptops, and important house documents. Next we grabbed our wedding album, baby pictures of the kids, and some random family photos. Finally, we packed enough clothes to last a few days. That was it: the car was full and time was running out. I threw in a few bottles of water and some treats for the dog, and then we got out of there.

It all felt so crazy and rushed. But once we had driven about an hour and were safely outside the reach of the fires, we had more time to contemplate our situation. Earlier that morning we had been obsessed with trying to take everything we owned with us in the car—now the only thing that mattered was that our family was together and out of harm's way. Without our even realizing it, our material possessions had become immaterial.

When the National Guard allowed us to return almost a week later, the scene was something out of a dooms-day movie. There was devastation everywhere and black smoke hung thick in the air. Fortunately, the houses in our neighborhood and the surrounding area were still standing. Our home was covered in soot, but the structure itself had not sustained any damage. Many people in nearby communities, however, were not as lucky.

That evening I spoke to a friend whose house had literally burned to the ground. With surprising composure, he articulated what I had been thinking about throughout the time we had been evacuated. "We had a lot of great times in our home over the years," he said. "We raised our kids there, we watched them grow up there, and we celebrated so many holidays and life events there. Make no mistake, we are sad that we lost our house. But at the same time we don't have any regrets because we'll always have our memories of the wonderful times we spent there. Not even a fire can take that away."

When you think about it, we really don't need most of the things we think we do. So much is just stuff that we've grown dependent on or have come to expect. In the end, our happiness will be measured by how we've lived our lives—not by the material possessions we've accumulated. Don't lose sight of the important things in life. Open your eyes and put your stuff in perspective.

Measure your happiness
by how you've lived
your life, not by the
material possessions
you've accumulated.

~ *What material possessions in your life would it be tough to live without?*

~ *What would life be like without this "stuff"?*

Live Your Vision

IF YOU'VE EVER been on an airplane, you probably knew exactly where you were going. You didn't just hop on board and say, "Let's see where we wind up." In life the mission is more ambiguous. We don't always know which direction to head, and occasionally we may question whether or not we're on the right course. Without a clear destination in mind, life is tough to navigate.

That was the way my wife and I felt when our first child was born. We were so excited to become parents, but we had no idea how to make everything work in terms of maintaining our careers, taking care of our newborn, and still having quality time together. My wife put her full-time job on hold to stay home with our daughter while I continued traveling for business and basically living out of a suitcase most of the week. When I got back from a trip, I just wanted to decompress and have quality family time before jetting off again. My wife, on the other hand, was totally exhausted from being up every night with the baby and just wanted to sleep or have a minute to herself. She loved being a mom but felt like she was doing it all alone and in the process losing her husband and professional identity. I loved being a dad and enjoyed my job but felt like I had become an absentee father. This was not the life we had envisioned.

One weekend my parents stayed with the baby while my wife joined me on a work trip to Toronto. On the plane ride we talked at length about how we wished life could be different. In our vision of the future, I was spending less time on the road and we were parenting more collaboratively. In addition to being a mother, my wife was working part-time. We were traveling together as a family and living life on our own terms. While this was a wonderful vision, it seemed far too idealistic and out of reach.

Midway through the flight, my wife unexpectedly asked, "What do you think about moving to Europe for a year? We could live our vision over there and have an incredible adventure as a family."

I thought she was kidding. "We have a new baby, a dog, a mortgage, two car payments, and limited finances," I reminded her.

"Those are indeed challenges," she replied. "But what if we could find a way to work it all out—would you do it?"

I knew she was serious, and as crazy as the idea sounded, I was excited to go if we could somehow work out the logistics and a way to afford it.

It took us less than a month to get our game plan together. By focusing on how to make our vision happen as opposed to why it couldn't happen, we were able to come up with creative solutions. For instance, we rented out our house and subleased our cars. My sister-in-law, who at the time was studying abroad in London, offered to help us with taking care of the baby. I worked out an arrangement with my clients so that I had to come back to the United States only a couple of days each month. Then we bought the cheapest one-way tickets to London we could find and set off with an infant for the most incredible year of our lives. We made the impossible possible by turning our vision into a reality.

During that time we traveled to almost two dozen countries in Europe and the Middle East. My daughter ate her first cookie in Venice, napped next to the Coliseum in Rome, learned to walk in Norway, chipped her tooth in Greece, went to the Wailing Wall in Jerusalem, visited the Great Pyramids in Egypt, and had a bite of the biggest pretzel ever at Oktoberfest in Munich. My wife got inspired and started planning her next career move. We truly lived our vision as a family and had no regrets. It was invigorating and unforgettable.

You don't have to move to a foreign country or travel abroad to start living your vision, but you do have to get clear on where you're headed. What do you want tomorrow to look like? What will it take to make that happen? Instead of focusing on the barriers to making your vision a reality, consider what success looks like in the absence of those barriers. Find innovative ways to change your current circumstances. Live your vision and leave your regrets behind. Don't just dream it; do it.

Don't just dream it; do it.

~ *What is your vision of the future for your life?*

~ *How will you make that vision a reality?*

Listen to Your Heart

PART OF HUMAN nature is trying to make sense of the world. To do this, we apply mathematical properties, the principles of cause and effect, deductive reasoning, scientific inquiry, the laws of physics, and other time-tested tools to provide insight into how and why things happen. Yet there is still a lot that we don't understand and can't easily reduce to logic or linear equations. For example, why do coincidences happen? What is luck? Does karma really exist?

When we can't explain something through science or logic, we instinctively call it a mystery, an anomaly, a miracle, magic, or fate. In essence, we are inclined to find a reason for everything that happens to us in life, even in the absence of rational explanation. This quest for meaning leads us not only to contemplate the random occurrences in our life but to consider acting on them as well. In other words, we must be open to listening to our heart and taking an unforeseen path in life when the opportunity presents itself—even though we have no guarantees about where that path will lead. This, of course, has implications for regrets: *if taking this path does not work out the way I had hoped, will I regret it?* Or alternatively, *if I don't take this path, will I regret not knowing where it would have led and possibly miss a life-changing opportunity?*

I encountered a defining moment like this while walking down the street with my friend Barry when I was twenty-three years old. As he and I came to a crowded intersection, I noticed a tow truck pulling up to a car parked in front of Moe's, a popular restaurant in town. Instantly my gaze turned to the girl who was leaning against the passenger door of the car with an embarrassed look on her face. She was a vision of beauty: vibrant, radiant, and full of life.

Call it love at first sight, but I was instantly overcome by a powerful, intuitive sensation that I was supposed to spend the rest of my life with this woman whom I had never met and hadn't even talked to yet. I tried to shrug off this irrational thought, but something deep inside me told me I would regret it if I didn't go up to her. Again I fought the urge as I then considered how much I would also regret it if I made a total fool of myself. It was too late—I was drawn to her like a magnet and within moments was trading casual hellos with her.

Just when I thought the conversation was over, she proceeded to spill the details of the unfolding drama. Apparently her friend, the driver of the vehicle, was so excited to find such a prime parking space in front of Moe's that she locked the keys in the car—with the car running! Her face lit up as she recounted the story, and we both laughed as my friend Barry, attempting to play tow truck driver's assistant, accidentally ripped the weather stripping off the car's driver side window. Somewhere during our five-minute dialogue, I realized that there really was something special about this girl and that I never wanted to leave her side. While I couldn't explain it logically in my head, my heart was telling me that it was simply meant to be.

The encounter ended with an exchange of business cards. We got to know each other better over the phone for the next couple of weeks, and then we went on our first date just down the street from the spot where we had met. The rest is history. More than twenty years later, I still look back in wonder: I literally met my future wife while walking down a random street. Was it just a chance occurrence? Was it destiny? Or was there some rational explanation? If I had arrived just ten minutes earlier or later—or if I had walked down a different street or not taken a walk at all—I may have never met her. All I know is that I'm glad I listened to my heart in the end.

Some things can't be explained by science or probability tables. We simply do not know everything that life has in store for us. But when seemingly random events occur, be cognizant of not only what they may mean but also what new paths they may present for you. In other words, be open to the possibilities you have yet to discover so you don't regret missing an opportunity that could change your life. Listen to your heart and see where it leads you.

Listen to your heart and see where it leads you.

~ When have you failed to listen to your heart and what was the result?

~ What is an example of a time when listening to your heart paid off?

Find Your Own Voice

SOCIAL PRESSURE IS an inescapable reality for all of us, regardless of whether we are teenagers or adults. It's the reason why we may feel compelled to wear a particular brand of clothing, use the latest buzzwords, or act a certain way to fit in. It also may be why we think it's important to live in a particular neighborhood, drive a specific kind of car, or be politically correct. Left unchecked, our efforts to conform can consume our lives and leave us with regrets.

What makes us so obsessed with blending in? What is the allure of being just like everyone else? When our goal in life is simply to gain the approval of others, we lose clarity on what we bring to the table as individuals. That was me in the seventh grade. I was young, impressionable, and lost. Everything that mattered to me had to do with hanging with the "in" crowd and trying to win their acceptance. I did what they did, said what they said, and adopted their interests as my own. The last thing I wanted to be seen as was different.

One day my English teacher asked me to stay after class. Terrified, I approached her desk once the bell had rung. "What did I do, Mrs. Madden?" I asked with apprehension.

Mrs. Madden, who was probably in her fifties and had a strikingly youthful and kind face, replied, "It's not what you did—it's what you haven't done." I was confused. "When I was reading the essay you wrote for our last assignment," she continued, "I kept thinking to myself, *This kid could be a writer someday. He has talent, but it's all bottled up inside.* If you ask me, you're just scared to let it all out."

I was dumbfounded. "I don't know what to say."

"Of course you don't," she said, smiling. "Like most students your age, you spend so much time trying to fit in that you lose your sense of identity in the process. It's hard to express yourself when you don't know who you are. You're different, you're unique, and you have a special gift for articulating your thoughts. You just don't realize it yet! That's why I want you to join the creative writing club I run after school. It'll help you find your voice."

I took Mrs. Madden's recommendation and showed up at the next meeting. I had no idea what to expect. When I walked into the room, it was a bit of a shock. Kids were strewn all over the place: some were sitting in beanbag chairs; others were lying on the floor. One of them even had a pillow and had taken off his shoes! All of them were busy writing in journals as "Carry On My Wayward Son" by Kansas, one of my favorite bands at the time, blared in the background. Mrs. Madden greeted me, then handed me a journal and told me to start writing.

"About what?" I asked her.

"About whatever you want," she said. "Find a place in the room and try closing your eyes. It will come to you."

At first I felt stupid and self-conscious sitting there on the floor with an empty journal in my hand and my eyes shut. *What if my friends looked in through the window and saw me?* "Relax," I heard Mrs. Madden say to me from across the room. I tried focusing on the music, and that helped calm me down. Then for some reason I started thinking about my Uncle Joe, whose funeral I had just attended over the weekend. He was someone that I loved very much and was really going to miss. That was it! Suddenly I had a flood of thoughts about what a great guy Uncle Joe had been, and I began writing. When I left the room an hour later, I had written my first poem.

From that point on, even through high school, when very few of my friends thought writing poetry and short stories was cool, I religiously attended Mrs. Madden's creative writing club. She taught me writing techniques, the art of creative expression, and most of all the importance of discovering who I was and having the courage to be that person without any regrets. I can still hear her telling me, "Find your authentic voice." That is exactly what I did.

Instead of sticking to the status quo, differentiate yourself from the masses. Resist the forces of conventionality and harvest your hidden talents. Live true to your core beliefs. Express your viewpoint even if it is unpopular. Follow your heart and pursue whatever taps your passion. Find your own voice and unleash your full potential.

Find your own voice and unleash your full potential.

~ What are some ways you feel pressured to conform to the status quo?

~ With this in mind, how can you still express your unique voice?

16

Speak Your Mind

WHEN MY DAUGHTER, Jessica, entered kindergarten, we found out the school had a "Books and Beyond" program where students received a special T-shirt and got to shake hands with the principal at the end of the year if they read a specified number of books. Since Jessica was a voracious reader, she was elated. Every night when we'd read books aloud before bedtime, she would ask, "Daddy, do you know what's going to happen in June?" Without waiting for an answer she'd exclaim, "Principal Stevens is going to shake my hand! He's really going to shake my hand, Daddy." She'd repeat this last line several times with great enthusiasm. By March, Jessica had already surpassed the program goal and was eagerly awaiting the end-of-year award ceremony.

On the day of the big event, Jessica insisted on wearing her party dress and fanciest shoes. She was so excited! My wife and I went early with her to find a good seat in the auditorium and had our cameras ready for the long-awaited handshake. Soon the assistant principal got up on stage and thanked all of the students for a job well done. Then she informed everyone that, unfortunately, Principal Stevens had a last-minute schedule conflict and that she would be shaking the award winners' hands in his place. The room grew silent and my daughter started crying. When her name was called, she wouldn't even look up as she walked over to the handshake line. It was a major letdown.

That night I couldn't sleep. I knew how disappointed my daughter was, and while experiencing a big letdown like this could perhaps be a teachable moment about the realities of life one day, right now my heart just hurt for her. More than anything, I felt that Principal Stevens needed to know how upset we were. But what good would that do? What's done was done. I also didn't want to sound like a big complainer, especially since my daughter would be spending the rest of her elementary career at this school. If I made a big deal of this, I might regret it for a long time. But if I didn't speak up, would I regret that even more?

The next day I went in to see Principal Stevens. He was in a meeting, but he stepped out for a moment to hear my concerns. After I told him the story, he looked shocked— it had never occurred to him that the handshake ritual would take on such great importance in the eyes of the students. Without further deliberation, he excused himself from the meeting and motioned for me to follow him as he headed for the lunchroom. When we got there he asked me to point out my daughter. "She's the one with the big bow," I said as I directed him across the room.

Principal Stevens made his way toward her through the sea of children who were now hanging all over him.

Upon reaching her seat, he got down on one knee and said, "Hi, Jessica, I'm Principal Stevens. I understand you've read a lot of books this year." My daughter looked up, astonished at how he knew this. "I'm sorry I missed the ceremony yesterday," he continued, "but I want you to know that I'm *very* proud of you and I'd like to shake your hand." With that, he gave her the biggest handshake ever and urged her to keep reading. To this day, I have never seen my daughter's face beam like it did at that particular moment.

The experience with Principal Stevens reaffirmed for me the importance of being assertive. If you don't let people know what you're thinking, don't expect them to read your mind. Share your concerns or apprehensions and release yourself from the regret of letting negative emotions stew over time. Get your feelings off your chest and you will feel more authentic and alive. Speak your mind so that others know where you stand.

Speak your mind so that others know where you stand.

~ *What is a current situation where you could do a better job of speaking your mind?*

~ *What are the pros and cons of doing so?*

Be True to What You Value Most

WE JUGGLE A lot of balls in life. But when we have too many balls in the air, some of them are bound to drop. For example, a few years ago I missed my son and daughter's first day of school because I was out of town on business. Up until that point, I had been there every year for our family's first-day-of-school tradition of getting up early with the kids, cooking a big breakfast for them, and then taking their pictures outside in the front yard. I had always put this date on my calendar way in advance, but this time I had to attend a client event that couldn't be rescheduled.

If you're a working parent, it's unrealistic to think that you will be present for every special moment in your child's life. However, one specific commitment I made to myself was that I'd always be there for my kids' first day of school. Telling them that I wasn't going to make it this time was heartbreaking for me. While I knew I had let them down, more than anything I was upset because I had let myself down.

No matter how many balls you have in the air, you have to put what's most important first if you want to live your life with no more regrets. This experience was a pointed reminder for me, and as a result, I made a personal commitment to focus more on prioritizing my family, my marriage, and my quality of life. While it is certainly difficult at times, thus far I've curtailed my work with clients that requires frequent travel and have been transforming my business to one that is primarily done electronically, locally, and remotely.

In addition, I now regularly play catch or kick the soccer ball around with my son after school, sit in on my daughter's electric guitar jam sessions, take more frequent family getaways, and do more of my share around the house. And as far as my kids' first day of school goes? Rest assured that I've been there every year since with omelet pan and camera in hand.

Every one of us has a set of personal values that help guide us through life, but sometimes those values come into conflict and we have to make tough decisions. A good question to ask yourself during those times is, "What matters most?" This will force you to prioritize your values such that one of them winds up at the top of the list. While your entire set of values is important—for instance, maintaining a strong work ethic, being financially independent, honoring commitments, being happy, staying in shape, and spending time with family—the key is to figure out which one is the *highest* priority for you. Once you know the answer, you may have to make some important and potentially difficult changes in your life that include sacrificing one priority for the another. In the end, though, you'll never look back with regret if you are being true to what you value most in life.

Be true to what you value most in life.

— *What or who in your life is your top priority?*

— *When does this priority conflict with other priorities, and how do you resolve those conflicts?*

18

Pursue Your Happiness

WE ALL HAVE a spot in life—a place in the world where we feel happier and more energized. When you're at your spot, you know it because it's where you feel at your very best just for the mere fact of being there. That was the case when I first stepped foot in San Diego at the age of twenty-one. The weather was perfect, the beaches were beautiful, and the vibe was one I can only describe as "surfer casual"—shorts and flip-flops were permanently in fashion and considered acceptable attire everywhere I went. As an added bonus, snow skiing was just two hours away. You could literally be on the slopes and then back in the waves on the same day! I kept thinking to myself, *I hope I live here one day.*

Sure enough, I came out to San Diego to pursue my happiness. It was there that I finished my formal education, and during that time I got married, started my career, and spent unforgettable times with friends. Both my wife and I felt like we had found our spot. But only after we moved away did this realization became clearer. While moving allowed us to focus on our professional goals and get back on our feet financially, we continually found ourselves yearning to be back in California.

Late one September evening after almost eight years of being away, we came to the conclusion that the time had come to reclaim our spot in San Diego. We missed being there and knew it was the place we wanted to raise our kids. However, we had some very real concerns. Would we be able to afford it? Would we be able to find new jobs? Would we still like it as much as we did before? The only thing we were certain of was that we definitely wanted to be there and if we stayed away any longer, we might regret it for the rest of our lives. After weighing the pros and cons, we decided to put our house on the market the next morning for the sake of pursuing our happiness.

Little did we know what would occur the following day: September 11, 2001. Suddenly selling a house and making a major life change seemed like a bad idea. But as disillusionment set in, it also helped clarify what we needed to do. If there was ever a time to pursue our happiness, that time was now when it felt like the world was falling apart all around us. We elected to stick with our plan and put up the For Sale sign. To our surprise, our house sold in only one week. Sadly, the people who bought it had just lost a family member in the World Trade Center tragedy. Just one month later we were back in San Diego, a spot that we have no intention of leaving any time soon.

When you pursue your happiness, you are making a statement that you are committed to living a life where you feel energized and inspired. This doesn't mean you have to move to a new city or make an abrupt change in your life but simply that you plan to follow your heart in the name of being happy. Whether it's pursuing a job at a company where you'd love to work, pursuing a relationship that you really want to develop, or pursuing a dream that you've put on hold, the quest to be happy is a cause worth fighting for. Pursue your happiness and see how the world looks brighter.

Pursue your happiness and see how the world looks brighter.

~ *How will you pursue your happiness over the next thirty days?*

~ *What challenges stand in the way, and how will you overcome them?*

PART FOUR

Stretch Yourself

19

Give It a Shot

FROM AN EARLY age we are taught that winning is important. But often we put so much pressure on ourselves to succeed that we become fixated on the prospect of failing. For instance, if you've ever interviewed for a job or tried out for a position on a team, think about the questions that went through your mind at some point: *What if they don't like me? What if I mess up? What if there are more-qualified candidates? What if they pick someone else?* Getting caught up in this negative thought process puts us at a competitive disadvantage because our attention is focused on what can go wrong as opposed to what can go right.

When we let our fears and doubts get in the way, it's easy to get psyched out and overwhelmed. At the extreme, our apprehension about the possibility of not achieving success may lead us to believe we shouldn't even try. In other words, if we don't take the risk of failing, then we know we can't fail. While this may make intuitive sense, the converse is also true: if we don't take the risk of failing, then we'll never give ourselves the chance to succeed. The result in either case is regret about what we could have, should have, or would have done—if only we'd had more confidence in ourselves or been less scared to try.

I remember when I was playing my third season of Little League baseball and my dad—who was also the team coach—asked me if I wanted to pitch.

"You mean in a real game?" I asked.

"Yes, in a real game," he replied.

"But I've never pitched before," I said.

"Right. So this will be a great way to get some experience," he said. "I'll teach you how, and then we'll practice until you get the hang of it."

I told him that the plan sounded good, although I was terrified inside.

For the next several weeks, my dad gave me pitching lessons. In an effort to alleviate my fears, he asked, "What's the worst thing that can happen?"

After giving it some thought, I replied, "I could walk every batter or get ten home runs hit off me and then we'd lose the game."

Then he said, "So if that's the *worst* thing that can happen, I'm not sure what's stopping you. You'll never know how good you can be unless you give it a shot."

I knew he was right, but I still felt unsure of myself.

The day of my pitching debut I was a total wreck. In my heart I really wanted to pitch, but in my head I kept seeing a disaster in the making. On the car ride to the game, I asked my dad to pull over. "I think I'm going to be sick," I said. He stopped on the side of the road and stepped out of the car with me as I got some fresh air.

Once I felt a little better, he asked, "Do you remember your first year in Little League when you learned how to hit a baseball?"

"Kind of," I said.

"Well, trust me when I tell you that for weeks you refused to even put on a batting helmet," he said. "You wanted to get on base but were scared to death of striking out or getting hit by a pitch."

The memory of this experience started to come back to me. "I remember now. You told me something about stepping up to the plate," I said.

"Yes," replied my dad as we said in unison: "*You can't get a hit unless you step up to the plate.*" We both laughed; then he said, "How about if we change the saying to '*You can't strike 'em out unless you get out there and start pitching*'?"

This resonated with me—if I didn't give it a shot, I'd never know how good I could be.

While the opposing team beat us pretty good that day, I managed to strike out a few batters. After that, I pitched for the rest of my Little League career. Even though I was not destined to play through high school, the experience did wonders for my confidence and was a lot of fun. Now I coach my own son, who is turning out to be quite a pitcher!

Get out of the trap of avoiding the risk of failure and get into the habit of taking a chance on success. Believe in yourself and trust your abilities. Put your best foot forward every time. Give yourself credit for trying and see what happens. Regardless of the outcome, you'll never regret that you had the guts to give it a shot.

Take the risk of failing
and give yourself the
chance to succeed.

~ *What have you avoided doing in your life
because you are afraid to fail?*

~ *What is the worst thing that would happen
if you failed?*

20

Trust Your Inner Strength

WE ARE ALL capable of doing and achieving more than we think is possible. Whether it's getting through tough times in our personal lives, hitting difficult deadlines and performance goals at work, or increasing the amount of repetitions and intensity in a workout, we can sometimes do what is seemingly impossible by simply putting our minds to it and pushing ourselves beyond our perceived limitations. But if we don't trust our inner strength, we may start to shy away from challenges, fail to realize our full potential, or give up on our dreams—all of which can be sources of regret. In the end, it comes down to whether or not we are willing to truly believe in ourselves and our abilities.

Case in point: several years ago I got the crazy idea that I was going to run a marathon. First you must understand that I am not a long-distance runner. Actually I'm not much of a runner at all—in a good month I might run one to two miles every couple of weeks. Plus I run *really, really* slow. So when I signed up on a whim for the Rock 'n' Roll Marathon just a couple of months before the race, it would be fair to assume that I was delusional in setting a personal goal of running 26.2 miles.

My training plan was simple: "Run more than I do right now." During the first week, I did a series of short runs every other day. Then over the weekend I decided to go for a career high eight-mile run to test my stamina. Suffice it to say that by mile five I thought I was going to die. For the next several days every part of my body ached and I could barely walk. Without further deliberation I put the marathon idea on the shelf. Some people are runners, but I was not. I had convinced myself that it just wasn't in the cards for me. In fact, I didn't give the race another thought until the night before the event. After a late evening out with friends who joked about how I had signed up for a marathon I was never going to run, a deep sense of guilt and remorse came over me—I had set a big challenge for myself and then chickened out because I didn't believe that I could really do it. I went to sleep with this weighing heavy on my mind.

The following morning I woke up at 5:30 a.m. without even setting my alarm clock. As I lay in the darkness, thinking how odd it was that I'd gotten up at the same time I would have needed to if I was actually going to run the marathon, two burning questions moved to the forefront of my thoughts: (1) *Will I regret it if I blow off this race?* and (2) *If I don't blow it off, do I have what it takes to finish it?* Certainly, not training, being severely out of shape, and staying out late the night before was not the best recipe for success. But as in the "Run, Forrest, run" scene in *Forrest Gump*, I suddenly had the inspiration to just start running. I quickly grabbed my jogging shoes and an old T-shirt and headed to the race.

The excitement of doing something this ridiculous carried me for the first half of the marathon. However, soon after that I hit the wall. My natural turtle-like pace became even slower, so much so that an elderly woman who was speedwalking the race with a cane actually passed me. At that point it occurred to me that I either had to give up and live with the regret of not completing the race or find the inner strength to push on. I felt sick to my stomach, dizzy, and winded. But with every ounce of energy I could muster, I made my legs move a little faster and told myself that I would regret it if I didn't keep going. While it took me six hours and thirteen minutes to complete the race— twice as long as it takes many runners—I succeeded in achieving my goal of making it to the finish line.

Running a marathon without training for it isn't the smartest idea in the world. But the experience proved to me that when we trust our inner strength, anything is possible. It also showed me that sources of regret such as underachieving, throwing in the towel too early, and underestimating ourselves are potentially avoidable. Whenever you are faced with a difficult challenge or an opportunity that seems out of reach, remember that each of us has the ability to conquer our perceived limitations and fears. Believe in yourself and your abilities, and most of all trust your inner strength.

When you trust your inner strength, anything is possible.

~ *What is a big challenge or difficult situation you are struggling with right now?*

~ *How can trusting your inner strength help get you through it?*

Get Out of Your Comfort Zone

MOST PEOPLE DON'T relish the opportunity to put themselves and others into uncomfortable situations. Tim Haggstrom is a bit different in that he makes his living doing it. You see, Tim's job is taking people up on high-elements ropes courses so that they can embrace their innermost fears and anxieties while suspended anywhere between thirty to fifty feet above the ground. The outdoor challenge exercises he facilitates—each designed to promote personal growth and development—get people to stretch beyond their comfort zones and serve as the impetus for positive behavioral change.

Tim is a firm believer that behaviors don't change if you keep doing exactly what you've always done and remain in an insulated environment. This has direct implications for regrets. For instance, if you always stay in your comfort zone, how can you grow and reach your full potential? In addition, failing to get out of your comfort zone may consequently make you risk averse and lead to the regret of feeling stifled, complacent, or bored with life.

On the other hand, getting out of your comfort zone can be a scary experience. But Tim would reaffirm that looking fear in the face is the only way to truly grow, gain genuine self-awareness, and see real behavior change.

So what does all this look like in application? Envision yourself climbing a thirty-foot telephone pole. Next you have to slowly raise your body until you are in a standing position on top of the pole—remember, it's a long way down. Your final challenge is to leap off the pole into midair and try to ring a bell that is hanging just out of reach in front of you. Although you are tethered by safety ropes the entire time, rest assured that most people are still scared to death!

Participating in such an initiative may bring up a number of issues depending upon the individual, the most obvious being a fear of heights. But beyond that, some powerful metaphors can be derived from each experience, many of which have direct tie-ins to dealing with previous regrets in life. In this case the metaphors might be "making the long climb to get to the top," "struggling to get over the edge" (once you're almost at the top), and "taking a leap of faith." By subsequently debriefing these issues after each ropes course activity, participants are able to acknowledge their fears and regrets as well as develop plans for moving forward.

While Tim's role is to facilitate personal challenge experiences that get others out of their comfort zones, he also is adamant about walking his talk and regularly putting himself through similar regimens to ensure he's come to terms with his lingering fears and past regrets in life. "At least once a year I make sure I really scare the crap out of myself," Tim says with full sincerity. "Last year it was extreme kayaking, the two years before that it was skydiving and rock climbing, and prior to that it was hot air ballooning, scuba diving, and hang gliding." Tim admits that currently he is focused on becoming a better public speaker, which in his opinion is the most terrifying thing he's ever done.

Getting out of your comfort zone gives you the opportunity to gain greater self-awareness and work through your past regrets. Realize that dealing with your fears is the key to producing behavioral change, whether on a ropes course or in real life. Take the initiative to face your demons and be cognizant of how you react. What do you notice about yourself? What can you learn from the experience? Get out of your comfort zone and see a new side of you.

Get out of your comfort zone and see a new side of you.

~ *What is a situation that would put you out of your comfort zone?*

~ *What fears would you have to face in that situation?*

22

Overcome the Obstacles

LIFE IS A bit like an obstacle course. As we try to move forward along the path to our goals, invariably something stands in our way. Sometimes it's a wall that seems insurmountable; other times it's a speed bump that slows us down or a detour that takes us in a new direction. Each time we encounter an obstacle, we must determine the smartest approach to overcome it without losing sight of our goals. Should we fail to get past the obstacle—especially when the stakes are high—we will surely experience regret.

I know that's how I felt when I was trying to complete the final hurdle in my formal education: a one-hundred-plus-page research project with a live presentation to a panel of professors at the end. The project was designed to take at least a full year to finish, but I needed to get it done in three months if I wanted to make the approaching graduation deadline. If I didn't finish, I'd have to wait one full additional year to graduate and have to pay another year's worth of tuition. To make matters worse, I had a new job lined up that was contingent upon my graduating. If I didn't complete the project in three months, there would be no graduation, no job, and a lot of regret.

My biggest obstacle in this case was fundamentally time—or so I thought. When I shared my three-month completion plan with my project advisor, however, his immediate response was "It would be a *herculean* task to get your project done by graduation. There's no way this will happen." It was apparent that my advisor, who was supposed to be my advocate, had now become an obstacle too. To overcome these obstacles, I spent the next three months working feverishly to complete my project while reassuring my advisor on a weekly basis that things were running on schedule despite his reluctance to support me in the process. On literally the last day possible to be eligible for graduation, I finished the written portion of the project and was ready to give my presentation to the faculty panel.

Gathered at the presentation were my classmates and some close friends, as well as my parents, who had traveled three thousand miles to be there for moral support. Moments before the proceedings started, the professor who was leading the panel pulled me aside and informed me that my parents would not be permitted in the room during the session. When I inquired why, the response I got was that it was not "customary" to have relatives attend, though there was no formal policy to that effect. Just when I thought the only obstacle left was my actual presentation, I now had another. While I wanted to protest,

I knew I'd regret it if somehow this negatively influenced the panel's evaluation of my presentation. Thus, I chose to overcome the obstacle by saying nothing and putting 100 percent of my focus back on the task in front of me. I will say, though, that having my parents barred from the room—and made to sit outside with ears against the door like eavesdropping children—definitely inspired me that much more to prevail.

For the next two hours I presented my project and fielded endless questions from the panel members. Then, after they deliberated for what seemed like forever, the head of the panel informed me that I had passed. It was an unforgettable feeling—finally I had overcome all of the obstacles that had been in the way of achieving my goal and this milestone in my education. I still have the photograph of the huge smile on my face at that particular moment.

The obstacles we face in life aren't always easy to overcome. They are a test of our determination, endurance, perseverance, and will. Refuse to let anything get in the way of completing the objectives you set for yourself, both at work or school and in your personal life. Say no to naysayers and keep your focus on the endgame. Be strategic, tenacious, and resilient. Overcome the obstacles and make it your mission to achieve your goals.

Overcome the obstacles
and make it your
mission to achieve
your goals.

~ *What is a major goal that you are currently working on, and what are the obstacles in the way?*

~ *How will you overcome them?*

23

Broaden Your
Cultural Perspective

MORE THAN EVER before, the saying "It's a small world"
rings true when it comes to being globally connected.
Whether in politics, environmental issues, military conflicts, technology, or the economy, there is a growing
awareness that what's going on in other parts of the world
can have a very real and immediate impact on our lives.
But despite the realization that we are a global community, the lens through which we view other people, their
customs, and their ways of life is still rather limited. For
instance, many of us proclaim to celebrate cultural diversity with only superficial knowledge of the cultures being
celebrated. From this standpoint, our perspective is myopic
and may in turn be a reason for regret.

The time is ripe to broaden our perspective on cultural diversity as part of our evolution as world citizens.
While this can be done in part by travel or study abroad,
it is also as simple as taking the initiative to expand our
awareness of the diverse cultural world that is closer to
home. For instance, two colleagues of mine, Joe and Susie,

have a long-standing ritual with a group of their friends from different cultural backgrounds where they celebrate each other's traditions and holidays together throughout the year. This includes learning more about their different religious faiths and even visiting each other's respective places of worship.

As an outgrowth of this process, last year Joe and Susie decided to hold an "international potluck" night where all of their friends brought food dishes that were indicative of their cultural heritages. They also were asked to prepare a list of interesting facts about their cultures of origin on note cards that they put next to their dishes. By the end of the evening, the group realized that more than twenty different cultures were represented among them and that they had all learned something new from the experience.

The international potluck was such a success that everyone in attendance agreed to make it a rotating monthly event where the host family got to pick the cultural theme and was responsible for coming up with a creative cultural dining and learning experience for the group. In just the first year, Joe, Susie, and their friends tasted ethnic foods from India, Korea, Brazil, Sweden, the Middle East, Ghana, Croatia, Morocco, Belgium, Jamaica, Bangladesh, and Singapore. They also learned songs, dances, folklore, history, and other interesting facts from each of these unique cultures.

Joe and Susie's ongoing practice of sharing their cultural customs and holidays with their friends continues to yield positive results: more education, less ignorance, a renewed appreciation for each other's differences, and lots of fun. It has also taken their friendships to a much higher level and has been enlightening for adults and children alike.

Don't go through life with blinders on. Avoid the regret of cultural closed-mindedness by forming your own opinions about other cultures through direct observation and experience instead of reliance on stereotypes and myths. Get curious and take the time to see others from a different point of view. In addition, recognize that the way you perceive cultural differences is only one viewpoint. Broaden your cultural perspective and appreciate the beauty of being different.

Broaden your
cultural perspective
and appreciate
the beauty of
being different.

~ How will you broaden your cultural
perspective?

~ What will you do to learn more about the
culturally diverse people around you?

24

Match Up with a Mentor

LIFE DOES NOT come with a user's manual. There are no detailed instructions, no twenty-four-hour help desks, and no blueprints to follow for becoming financially successful, happily married, socially competent, or personally content. Without clear direction in life, we can easily become frustrated, lost, aimless, discouraged, or stuck in a rut, which in turn can be a source of regret. So how do we avoid this trap and the feelings of regret that come with it as we seek to achieve our goals?

Beyond relying on trial and error, risk taking, and raw creativity to get ahead in life, a viable strategy that is easy to put into practice is to match up with a mentor—someone who is a trusted guide, advisor, and counselor. Mentors impart knowledge, help us develop our skills, and teach us how to avoid regrets in life. They shed light on the big picture of life and share stories of how they got to where they are. They help us network and open new doors. They share tricks of the trade and serve as sounding boards when we are stuck or confused. They provide coaching and fresh perspectives. Ultimately, mentors can accelerate our learning curve and reduce some of the ambiguity in life.

An amazing mentor in my life has been Ken Blanchard, a renowned author and speaker whom I met early in my career. In college I saw a video in which he talked about the key principles from his book *The One Minute Manager*, and as a result I was inspired to apply for an internship position at his company while I was finishing school. At the age of twenty-one, I joined his firm as a part-timer making about four dollars an hour. But what I learned from Ken was worth more than I could ever put a price tag on. He taught me to see the potential in every human being and to have a clear vision for the future. He taught me to focus on catching people doing things right as opposed to ambushing them when they did something wrong. He also taught me that I need to celebrate the small wins in life and that humility didn't mean thinking less of myself, just thinking about myself less. In a nutshell, he taught me some of the secrets to living a life free of regrets.

Ken once brought me into a company board meeting as a learning opportunity and had me sit at the table with the executives. Instead of positioning me as a young intern who would simply be an observer, he welcomed me as part of the team for the day and encouraged me to actively participate in the meeting. This helped build my confidence and prompted the group members to treat me as one of their own, even though I was half their age and new to the corporate world. It also taught me that setting the right tone and making people feel respected—regardless of their job title or experience—goes a long way. Matching up with Ken as a mentor helped clarify the path I wanted to take as both a professional and a person in terms of my values and behaviors, and it allowed me to avoid the regret of taking a lifetime to figure that out.

So how do you match up with a mentor? Where do you start? The process is actually quite simple and straightforward: identify people whom you think you can learn a lot from and then solicit their interest in mentoring you. In other words, be assertive and ask them for what you want. The script goes something like this and takes only a few seconds to deliver: "Hi, Pat. I'm impressed with what you've done with your life/career and I think I could learn a lot from you. Would it be okay if I called or e-mailed you from time to time to pick your brain and get some advice?" What do you think the person is going to say, "How dare you insult me like that"? Highly unlikely! You can bet that most people will be flattered by the request and will be more than willing to serve in some advisory capacity—you simply have to ask.

Take the initiative to match up with a mentor. Seek out people who are willing to show you the ropes. Observe them in action and take note of how they operate. Have them share with you what they've learned from both their successes and their failures. Match up with a mentor and learn the secrets of life from someone who has already been down that road.

Match up with a mentor
and learn the secrets
of life from someone
who has already been
down that road.

— *In what area of your life would you benefit from a mentor?*

— *Whom will you ask to serve in this role?*

PART FIVE

Be a Force of Goodness

Keep an Open Mind

THREE WEEKS BEFORE my wife and I were married, her grandfather died of an aneurism. Just one month prior he had sent us pictures of his new wedding tuxedo that unfortunately he would never get to wear. We were devastated. Grandpa Phil was a great man whom everyone adored—he was a well-known physician in a small town in upstate New York, an accomplished photographer, and an all-around good guy. He looked like a big teddy bear, and he reminded me a lot of my own grandfather, who had long since passed.

The day before his funeral, we had to sort through Grandpa Phil's belongings to see what family members wanted to keep and what they wanted to give away. He had a large house, so we divided up the task by rooms and I got the basement. While weeding my way through the clutter, I found a dusty old trunk that looked like it hadn't been touched in years. I opened it and found hoards of files, each marked with a brief description of what the folder contained. Most were filled with photographs that

Grandpa Phil had taken of his family and grandchildren over the years. However, one file in particular that caught my eye had only "1934" written on the label. Inside was an old, yellowed clipping from the local newspaper. Intrigued, I sat down and gave the article a quick skim.

The story was about a court case where a man was actually sued by his own parents. He had gone to study medicine in Edinburgh, Scotland, in the late 1920s because at the time many medical schools in the United States would not accept Jewish students. Although his parents had readily provided some financial support for his academic endeavor abroad, they had a change of heart when he married a non-Jewish Scottish woman whom he had met while at school. His parents disowned them both and then sued him for all of the money they had invested in his medical education. Moreover, after his wedding day, his mother and father held a traditional ceremony of mourning for him as if he were dead. The man eventually prevailed in an extended legal battle, but his parents never talked to him again. He and his wife, and subsequently his children and grandchildren, were permanently cut off from his parents and relatives, many of whom lived in neighboring towns.

Only after I reread the article a couple of times did I realize that the man in the story was Grandpa Phil. I was struck by the regret that his parents must have experienced at some point for never seeing their son's family grow up and for never being a part of their grandchildren's and great-grandchildren's lives. I also tried to imagine how hard it must have been for Grandpa Phil and his family to live in such isolation; surely it must have been a source of regret for them as well.

People may look different, act different, or believe in different things. But that doesn't make them any worse than us—or us any better than them. When we reject others simply because they are different, we deny them the respect they deserve as human beings and make a statement about our own character in the process. We also miss out on the opportunity to get to know what they have to offer as individuals. This sense of "never knowing what could have been," along with the narrow-mindedness and implicit arrogance that go with it, are viable reasons for regret that can easily be avoided if we work harder to keep an open mind.

Make it a habit to set aside your preconceived notions and assumptions about others. Give them the benefit of the doubt and strive to be more accepting of their differences. Think of how you would like to be treated if you were in their shoes, and then treat them accordingly. When you keep an open mind, people just may surprise you and do great things.

Give people a chance
to shine—they just
may surprise you
and do great things.

~ *What is an example of when you've prejudged someone, only to regret it later?*

~ *How will you give people a chance to shine going forward?*

26

Love Unconditionally

THE WORD UNCONDITIONAL means "without limitations." Perhaps a more complete definition of the term, though, is "without limitations and without regrets." When you love others unconditionally, you acknowledge their shortcomings and do not judge them. They may frustrate you, disappoint you, test your patience, and at times drive you crazy, but you never regret loving them because you've made a conscious choice to accept them for who they are and are willing to embrace the heartburn that may come with that decision. This is different from conditional love, where failing to meet certain expectations or provisions in a relationship can be a major source of regret that may ultimately end the relationship.

Someone I love unconditionally is Billy, my Little Brother. When I joined the Big Brothers program back in 1991, he had just turned ten and was living on welfare with his mom and sisters. Growing up as an African-American young male in a neighborhood with primarily people of different ethnicities was difficult for him and often resulted in physical confrontations. Crime was rampant, drive-by shootings were frequent, and pressure to join a gang was persistent. Yet much of that seemed to fade away when Billy and I were together.

My commitment to Billy was that I would always be his Big Brother and love him unconditionally, regardless of what happened to him in life. This got put to the test on many occasions in the years that followed, whether he had difficulty with making grades at school, holding a job, managing his money, or staying out of trouble. "I'm here to help you, not judge you," I'd say, but the disappointments he'd experienced growing up and his chronic issues with self-esteem made it hard for him to believe I'd really always be there for him.

One day I got a call from Billy and it sounded like he had hit rock bottom. In his own words, he had failed everyone including himself—he had no job, no money, and nowhere to go. My wife and I asked him to come live with us and told him he could stay as long as he wanted. For the better part of a year, Billy took up residence at our house while he worked on turning his life around. We gave him the run of the place, helped him get his résumé together, and continued to reinforce that we were there to support him in good times and bad.

Upon returning home with our kids one afternoon, we found Billy's packed suitcase by the door to his room. Billy was sitting inside on the sofa bed with his head buried in his arms. After a bit of coaxing, he showed his face but couldn't speak. Then he slowly got up and pointed to where he had been sitting. A huge hole had been burned through the sofa cushion. "I was late for work and forgot to turn off the iron," he said, mortified. "You've put so much trust in me and now look how I've blown it."

I was floored—did Billy really think we'd kick him out of the house over this? I gave him a big hug and said, "When I told you that I unconditionally loved you, I meant it and I'll never regret it. And by the way, it will take a lot more than ruining a couch to get rid of me." Billy managed to smile and together we unpacked his bag.

Loving someone unconditionally requires tolerance, dedication, acceptance, and patience, even if this person occasionally lets you down or falls short of your expectations. It also requires making sure you don't get taken advantage of in the process, meaning that mutual respect is still important. Take a moment to think about a current or past relationship and evaluate how well it fits the definition of unconditional—this could be a relationship with a friend, a lover, a boss, a coworker, a sibling, a parent, a child, a relative, or even a pet. Would you describe this relationship as one without limitations and regrets?

The challenge with unconditional love is being able to withhold the urge to judge people or to try to force them to change and instead learning how to accept them for who they are. Once you embrace the reality that what you see may be exactly what you get, being in that relationship will no longer be a source of regret. Love unconditionally and experience the beauty of loving someone without limitations or regrets.

Love unconditionally
and experience the
beauty of loving
someone without
limitations or regrets.

~ *Whom will you strive to love more unconditionally in your life?*

~ *What factors make your love for this person conditional right now?*

27

Take a Mulligan

I AM NOT an avid golfer. Actually I'm what some people would refer to as a hack—you'd best take cover when I'm at the tee. Admittedly, I have no business playing golf around people who take it seriously. But I do have a great appreciation for various aspects of the sport, one of the most intriguing of which is "taking a mulligan." Even if you don't play the game, the concept is easy enough to understand: a mulligan is a "second chance" that is typically offered in informal golf when you hit a bad shot. In other words, you are given the opportunity to hit your shot over again and the first one is forgiven.

Taking a mulligan in golf has many parallels to daily life. When we hurt people's feelings, we apologize and can take a mulligan if they give us the chance to make it up to them. When we disappoint people, we can take a mulligan if they give us the chance to regain their trust. When we fail or fall short of others' expectations, we can take a mulligan if they give us the chance to retrench and give it another try. Likewise, taking a mulligan is an opportunity we can give to others when they go astray, make mistakes, or don't live up to the mark.

Not too long ago I had the chance to chat with Wally Armstrong, who cowrote *The Mulligan: A Parable of Second Chances*, a wonderful story that uses golf as a metaphor for life. After Wally shared the philosophy behind his book, I asked him, "Aren't there situations when a mulligan isn't warranted—does everyone *really* deserve a second chance?"

"I sure hope so," Wally responded, "though I know it's tough for a lot of people to think that way. Sometimes it's hard to see the good in everyone."

"But aren't some acts unforgivable?" I continued, trying to clarify my point.

"That's a tough one," Wally replied. "What's clear to me is that we are all capable of doing wrong to varying degrees. However, we are also capable of doing right once we see the error of our ways. I'm personally a fan of giving people second chances. But true forgiveness—the ultimate expression of letting someone take a mulligan—can only come from our hearts."

Wally's statement was powerful and thought provoking. Did I have enough compassion in my heart to let someone take a mulligan after doing me wrong or breaking my trust? Could I simply let it slide and move on without being bitter? I reflected on a long-term friendship I had ended several years ago because forgiveness did not feel like an option. At the time, I was very hurt and angry. Yet now time had passed and a part of me regretted not having buried the hatchet with my friend. On a whim I decided to give him a call. While the conversation was a little uncomfortable at first, it was not long before we were laughing and recounting old times as we caught up with each other's lives. At some point in the discussion we talked about the circumstances that had driven us apart. By letting my friend take a mulligan, both of us were able to put the past behind us and move forward. Once I forgave him in my heart, it not only resolved my feelings of regret but also opened up the opportunity for us to start rebuilding our friendship.

A mulligan is a gift you give people when you think they deserve another shot. It says you acknowledge that they are fallible and that you have the compassion in your heart to forgive them. It also helps alleviate the regret you may have felt if you left the situation unresolved. We can only hope that others will return the favor the next time we make a mistake. But we also need to learn to offer ourselves a mulligan—at times we can be harder on ourselves than we need to be. While we may do something wrong the first time, taking a mulligan provides a second chance to make it right.

Give people the
gift of forgiveness
and a second chance
to make things right.

~ *When in your life have you given someone a second chance to make things right?*

~ *When has someone given you a second chance?*

Do the Right Thing

MANY YEARS AGO I attended a workshop on choice-based living in which the lecturer talked about how we can improve our sense of efficacy in life by "making decisions, big or small, in good conscience." After the session I asked him to clarify what he specifically meant by that. "The bottom line is that when you are choosing one course of action over another in life, always do the right thing," he said. "'The right thing,'" he continued, "is subject to individual interpretation, which is why you should let your conscience be your guide." Within the context of regrets, then, the definition of "the right thing" is perhaps best articulated as "the choice you won't regret."

Two people that have further stimulated my thinking around this topic are Nicole and Matt Benak. Not long after they had their first two children, a girl and a boy, the Benaks adopted a baby girl from Ethiopia. To their surprise, some of their friends couldn't imagine why they had chosen to adopt when seemingly they could just have more children on their own. This feedback was especially difficult for Nicole and Matt to absorb since they felt strong in their belief that they were doing the right thing for their family as well as for the baby in this case.

"We felt so incredibly blessed to be able to make this little girl a part of our family," Matt reflected. "Plus, when you realize that there are literally millions of orphan children throughout Africa as well as in other parts of the world, it just makes the decision to adopt an easy one for us."

Nicole added, "For us to bring another child into the world when there are so many children who are in dire need of a family seems like a choice that we would have regretted. We adopted our child because for us personally, it was the right thing to do and ultimately a win-win decision for all of us. In other words, as able and willing parents we were ready to expand our family, and by the same token, this orphan child needed a home and a loving family who wanted to take care of her."

A year later Nicole and Matt decided to adopt another child from the same agency in Ethiopia, this time a five-year-old boy.

The Benaks are not only an inspiration but also an example of how doing the right thing can be grounded in the principle of making choices in good conscience. As such, their choices are ones they won't soon regret.

Doing the right thing is about being able to live with your decisions in every part of your life. When faced with choosing one course of action over another, use your conscience as a guide. Ensure that your decision is one that you'll feel proud of and can readily stand behind. When you do the right thing, you'll never regret what you've done.

When you do the right thing, you'll never regret what you've done.

~ What is an example of when doing the right thing was not an easy decision for you?

~ What made the decision difficult?

Strive to Be Selfless

BEFORE MY WIFE and I decided to start trying to have children, we agreed that we should first get a dog. A few weeks after that discussion I surprised my wife with a seven-week-old Border collie mix puppy that had been rescued by the local shelter. While the shelter staff had named her Runtley because she was the runt of a litter of thirteen brothers and sisters, we decided to call her Scruffy instead based on her disheveled yet undeniably cute appearance.

Almost immediately we realized that while we were in love with the idea of having a dog, we were in way over our heads. Scruffy chewed through the linoleum floor in the kitchen, tore up the floorboards, mutilated the couch, and ate all of the doorstops. She regularly urinated on the carpet and howled all night long in her cage unless we let her come in and sleep in our bed. As much as we hated to admit it, we started to regret our decision to become dog parents.

One night after Scruffy had ripped up the new flowers we'd just planted in the backyard, my wife and I had a serious discussion regarding what to do about her. "Maybe we should return her to the shelter," I said.

"Or we could give her away to a family who could take better care of her," my wife added.

But almost as soon as the words came out of our mouths, we felt guilty and embarrassed. After all, Scruffy was just a puppy doing what puppies typically do. Why were we acting so surprised then? We were treating our dog like she was a nuisance and an inconvenience instead of recognizing that she was a puppy who simply needed our help to learn and feel loved. We were being selfish as opposed to selfless, which we realized was the true source of our regret about Scruffy.

The conversation ended with a mutual resolve to put our self-interest aside and make a more concerted effort to focus on Scruffy's needs. We started by taking her to obedience classes at the local pet shop and by working harder at getting her house trained. We took her on walks more often and bought her a doggy bed that we permanently put in our room. From that point on, we had no more regrets about our decision to get a dog or the decision to keep her. By being a little more selfless and patient, we were able to love and care for Scruffy for the entire fourteen years she was with us, even when she got sick at the end. The day we had to put her down—which was one of the saddest days of my life—I knew that we were thinking of what *she* needed at that point, which was to be free from pain. I will never forget holding Scruffy in my arms until she took her last breath and was finally at peace.

Strive to be selfless by putting your self-interest aside so that you can better understand and focus on the interests of others. Beyond taking care of a pet, this applies to raising a child, playing on a team, being a partner in a relationship, working in an organization, and being a good friend. To avoid the regret of being selfish, self-absorbed, and self-serving, consider others' needs as well as your own. Shift your focus outward instead of inward. When you strive to be selfless, you don't think less of yourself, you just think about yourself less.

Strive to be selfless—
don't think less
of yourself, just think
about yourself less.

— *With whom in your life would you like to be more selfless?*

— *What are some steps you can take to do this?*

30

Make the World a Better Place

IN A WORLD where the news headlines are monopolized by war, death, abuse, destruction, crime, tragedy, and scandal, it is refreshing once in a while to hear good news. Every now and then we come across accounts of people who have served as positive role models, done something constructive for their communities, donated their time or money, performed random acts of kindness, or even saved lives. Their stories inspire us and momentarily give us hope that the human spirit can still conquer. They also remind us that each of us can make a difference by doing our part to make the world a better place.

Two such people I know are Dave and Flo Wagner, who have spent most of their adult lives helping people make a better life in impoverished countries around the world. In their twenties, the Wagners did their first tour in the United States Peace Corps in Africa. Since then they have been actively committed to promoting entrepreneurship and educating parents about HIV/

AIDS in developing nations throughout Southeast Asia, Eastern Europe, and Africa, including war-torn regions like Ethiopia and Darfur.

Even after raising a large family and running successful businesses of their own, Dave and Flo—who are now in their sixties—dedicate months and years at a time to traveling to remote villages for the sole purpose of assisting people in need. Making the world a better place has become their life's work—it is how they define themselves as human beings. They receive no monetary rewards or public accolades. Yet this is what they see themselves doing for as long as they are physically able to do it. Doing anything else would create a huge void in their lives that would inevitably lead to regret.

Making the world a better place means being a force of goodness. It means being a giver, not a greed monger. It means shining your light on others without looking for something in return. It means being a "mensch"—a person who does good deeds—which in some cultures is considered the highest compliment you could ever pay someone. Consider the extent to which you are a force of goodness. Do you go out of your way to make other people's lives better? Do you volunteer or actively support a positive cause? Do you do your part to take care of the environment and reduce the amount of recyclable waste that goes to landfills? Do you reach out to others in need?

Making the world a better place does not have to be an overly complex or time-consuming process. Help out a friend who is hurting. Donate your extra "stuff" to charity. Visit the elderly. Show compassion to a total stranger. Make the commitment to recycle. Let people know that they are loved. Go beyond the call of duty. Leave your legacy by making the world a better place.

Leave your legacy by making the world a better place.

~ *What do you already do to make the world a better place?*

~ *How will you improve on that?*

Next Steps

REGRETS ARE THE things we do that we wish we hadn't done *and* the things we fail to do that we wish we had done, both of which result in unhappiness, disappointment, or remorse.

None of us want to look back on life with regrets about what we should have or could have done differently. Each of the thirty key messages in the chapters you've just read— whether a component of "Get Out of Your Rut," "Take Nothing for Granted," "Aim for Authenticity," "Stretch Yourself," or "Be a Force of Goodness"—has worked for me in my own life, and my sincere hope is that at least a few of them will work for you in your life too. Remember, just one story or idea that has clicked for you can create the insight and inspiration to help you truly start living a life with no more regrets.

Following are some immediate next steps you can take:

1. Ask the following two questions *each* time you need to make a decision:

- Will I have regrets if I do it (or don't do it)?
- Will I avoid having regrets if I do it (or don't do it)?

2. Create your No More Regrets! Game Plan for the next thirty days. In the following section I've provided an easy-to-use tool to get you started on this. Commit to making your Game Plan a reality and in just one month you'll have greater happiness and meaning in your life, career, and relationships.

3. Join me and a growing community of enthusiastic readers on Marc's Blog at http://www.no-more-regrets.com. Hear how others are putting their No More Regrets! Game Plans into practice, learn about their struggles and successes, and share your own stories as you work on having no more regrets in your life.

4. Recommend this book to people in your life who you believe will benefit from it. Let them know which chapters made you think of them. Encourage them to develop their own No More Regrets! Game Plan and share yours with them. Support each other as you put your Game Plans into action.

5. If you participate in a book club or reading group, make *No More Regrets! 30 Ways to Greater Happiness and Meaning in Your Life* required reading. Contact

me via the official book Web site, http://www
.no-more-regrets.com, and I will e-mail you a set
of engaging discussion questions that you can use
to debrief the book with your group.

I hope these ideas are helpful. Rest assured that I will
continue to offer more success strategies and tools at http://
www.no-more-regrets.com, so please check back · frequently. Living your life with no more regrets is a goal
within reach—if you make it your focus, I am confident
you will notice a positive difference in your life almost
immediately. Embark on your No More Regrets! journey
today and let me know how it goes!

The No More Regrets! Game Plan

CREATE YOUR OWN No More Regrets! Game Plan to help you get a clear strategy for taking action. Start today by filling in the boxes below:

> I. What is a past regret in your life that you would like to resolve or a regret that you would like to avoid going forward? Why?
>
> Your regret: _____
>
> _____
>
> _____
>
> Why resolve or avoid this regret going forward?
>
> _____
>
> _____
>
> _____
>
> _____
>
> _____

II. What specific chapters and/or key messages in the book will help you resolve or avoid this regret going forward?

1. _____

_____

_____

_____

_____

2. _____

_____

_____

_____

_____

3. _____

_____

_____

_____

_____

III. What specific steps will you take to apply the focus of these chapters and/or key messages over the next thirty days?

1.

2.

3.

IV. **Thirty days from now, what will be different or better in your life as a result of putting these specific steps into action?**

1.

2.

3.

V. How will you hold yourself accountable for putting these steps into action? Whom can you ask to support you in the process?

1. _____

2. _____

3. _____

Giving Back

The No More Regrets! Giving Club is committed to providing books for free to organizations that are dedicated to helping people live happier and more meaningful lives. Join the Giving Club—it's an incredible way to be a force of goodness by using a "pay-it-forward" approach to spreading the positive message of *No More Regrets!* to literally thousands of people through your in-kind book donations to a charitable organization or nonprofit of your choice. Current donation sites include literacy organizations, fun runs, churches, synagogues, fraternity and sorority foundations, counseling services centers, community-based nonprofit organizations, treatment programs, hospitals, youth camps, and more.

For more information about the No More Regrets! Giving Club and how to join, e-mail GivingClub@no-more-regrets.com or visit www.no-more-regrets.com.

About the Author

Photo by Corinne Jamieson

DR. MARC MUCHNICK is a leading authority on human behavior who is on a mission to help people live life with no more regrets. His last book, *The Leadership Pill* (co-authored with Ken Blanchard), was named on the *Wall Street Journal, BusinessWeek*, and Amazon.com best-seller lists, has sold over 125,000 copies, and has been translated into eighteen languages worldwide.

Beyond being an engaging author, Marc has been an online professor and research mentor for over fourteen years in the doctoral and masters of business administration programs at Capella University's School of Business and Technology. He has chaired over seventy doctoral dissertations and taught over 150 courses in his academic career.

In addition, Marc is a sought-after motivational speaker, life coach, and consultant. He is also the founder of People First Group, LLC, a consulting firm servicing leading organizations including start-ups, small and medium-sized businesses, and Fortune 500 companies, such as Dell Computers, Sony, Invitrogen, Hilton Hotels, Delta Air Lines, McDonald's, AT&T Wireless, Fidelity Investments, IBM, Bayer, Boeing, Estée Lauder Companies, Cox Communications, Zales Jewelers, Petco, Marriott Hotels, JC Penney, Republic Waste Services, Symantec, National Car Rental, the Federal Reserve Bank, Cigna Healthcare, the Central Intelligence Agency, Aveda Salons, the University of Nebraska, and the Ritz-Carlton Hotels.

Marc lives in San Diego with his wife, two children, and dog Cali and is in his nineteenth year as a Big Brother in the Big Brothers/Big Sisters Program of America. Marc is a leader, a motivator, a coach, an educator, a problem solver, and an individual who inspires others by walking his talk.

Berrett–Koehler
Publishers

Berrett-Koehler is an independent publisher dedicated to an ambitious mission: *Creating a World That Works for All*.

We believe that to truly create a better world, action is needed at all levels—individual, organizational, and societal. At the individual level, our publications help people align their lives with their values and with their aspirations for a better world. At the organizational level, our publications promote progressive leadership and management practices, socially responsible approaches to business, and humane and effective organizations. At the societal level, our publications advance social and economic justice, shared prosperity, sustainability, and new solutions to national and global issues.

A major theme of our publications is "Opening Up New Space." Berrett-Koehler titles challenge conventional thinking, introduce new ideas, and foster positive change. Their common quest is changing the underlying beliefs, mindsets, institutions, and structures that keep generating the same cycles of problems, no matter who our leaders are or what improvement programs we adopt.

We strive to practice what we preach—to operate our publishing company in line with the ideas in our books. At the core of our approach is stewardship, which we define as a deep sense of responsibility to administer the company for the benefit of all of our "stakeholder" groups: authors, customers, employees, investors, service providers, and the communities and environment around us.

We are grateful to the thousands of readers, authors, and other friends of the company who consider themselves to be part of the "BK Community." We hope that you, too, will join us in our mission.

A BK Life Book

This book is part of our BK Life series. BK Life books change people's lives. They help individuals improve their lives in ways that are beneficial for the families, organizations, communities, nations, and world in which they live and work. To find out more, visit **www.bk-life.com**.

Berrett–Koehler
Publishers

A community dedicated to creating
a world that works for all

Visit Our Website: www.bkconnection.com

Read book excerpts, see author videos and Internet movies, read
our authors' blogs, join discussion groups, download book apps, find
out about the BK Affiliate Network, browse subject-area libraries of
books, get special discounts, and more!

Subscribe to Our Free E-Newsletter, the *BK Communiqué*

Be the first to hear about new publications, special discount offers,
exclusive articles, news about bestsellers, and more! Get on the list
for our free e-newsletter by going to **www.bkconnection.com**.

Get Quantity Discounts

Berrett-Koehler books are available at quantity discounts for orders
of ten or more copies. Please call us toll-free at (800) 929-2929 or
email us at bkp.orders@aidcvt.com.

Join the BK Community

BKcommunity.com is a virtual meeting place where people from
around the world can engage with kindred spirits to create a world
that works for all. BKcommunity.com members may create their own
profiles, blog, start and participate in forums and discussion groups,
post photos and videos, answer surveys, announce and register for
upcoming events, and chat with others online in real time. Please join
the conversation!

© **Mixed Sources**
Product group from well-managed
forests, controlled sources and
recycled wood or fiber
www.fsc.org Cert no. SW-COC-003925
© 1996 Forest Stewardship Council
FSC